Fashioned into a Bow

Fashioned into a Bow

How resolute, heroic women earned the George Medal

Major D. V. Henderson, GM

The Pentland Press
Edinburgh – Cambridge – Durham – USA

First published in 1995 by
The Pentland Press Ltd
1 Hutton Close
South Church
Bishop Auckland
Durham

ISBN 1-85821-273-1

Typeset by Carnegie Publishing, 18 Maynard St., Preston
Printed and bound by Antony Rowe Ltd., Chippenham

Article 7 of the Warrant states, *inter alia*

'Provided that when the Medal is worn by a woman it may be worn on the left shoulder suspended from a ribbon of the same width and colour fashioned into a bow.'

Dedicated to my late wife, Maisie
(Wing Offr. M. T. Russell, PMRAFNS (ret'd))
for her patience, steadfast understanding,
encouragement and love.

With heartfelt thanks to those individuals or organisations, world-wide, who have volunteered information or answered queries, often at great length. Without this help this book could not have got off the ground and that would have been a great pity for these brave individuals deserve recognition on the same scale as their brethren.

Contents

Foreword

by Rear Admiral M. Morgan-Giles DSO, OBE, GM, DL

THIS book is first and foremost a wonderful tribute to women – to all women who have ever been.

Major Henderson has gathered together some amazing stories about their wartime achievements.

But war is Man's business: Women's mission is to create life and to nurture it.

So it is all the more remarkable that under the compulsion of total war women have shown such magnificent cool courage and enterprise as the author records – in the Blitz, as agents working in enemy- occupied countries, etc. etc.

Men can shine in immediate battlefield situations – in hot blood, and supported by shoulder-to-shoulder comradeship with other men. But women, some of whom might be frightened of a mouse in their kitchen, have bravely and often alone endured terrible prolonged dangers and tortures as recounted in this book, and doubtless in many other situations which have no memorial.

In doing so they have silently contributed more to the post-war improvement in the status of womanhood than all the shrill protests of their 'feminist' sisters.

We men may feel guilty that such a small proportion of George Medals have been awarded to women – a point made by the author in his Introduction. But personally, I rather doubt whether women spend much time worrying about this: they are too sensible.

In any case it may be that any woman who has given birth to a child deserves a medal – we men should ponder that, too!

The George Medal is essentially to recognise achievements not in the face of the enemy – in other words which do not involve killing.

It is for future generations to decide whether women should be armed and incorporated into the conventional fighting forces. That they could do so, if necessary, and do so bravely and successfully, any reader of this book must agree; but whether morally they should be put in such positions is another thing.

Major Henderson GM, who himself knows all about bravery, has diligently produced a splendid book. He throws light upon an interesting and much neglected chapter in the history of our nation. Men and women of all generations will feel humbled, but inspired and uplifted by reading it.

Introduction

For as long as human endeavour has been possible man has responded to emergency situations involving companions or colleagues. Such predicaments may have resulted from combat conditions on land or sea or in the air or from a chance combination of non-operational factors.

Eventually it became the practice to recognise outstanding acts of bravery (also variously identified as valour, gallantry, heroism, courage) with a wide selection of awards – titles, honours, money, trophies (notably presentation watches), orders, decorations or medals.

As far as British (and Empire/Commonwealth) bravery awards are concerned, one area of confusion relates to those orders which were awarded for both distinguished service and bravery, two examples of which are the Order of the Bath and the Distinguished Service Order. Up to 1974 another case in point was the Order of the British Empire (and its Medal) up to the class of 'Commander' although from 1958 bravery was signified by the addition of an emblem of two (crossed) silver oak leaves to the ribbon.

The horrific years of the First World War saw a dramatic increase in the range of medals and decorations available to reward gallantry in *action* against an enemy but, even at its end, the choice of analogous awards for other forms of high courage was minimal. In the United Kingdom and British Empire it was limited to the Albert Medal, the Edward Medal, the Sea Gallantry Medal and to those in the gift of private institutions such as the Royal Humane Society.

Along with the Edward Medal (for Mining or Industry) most of the private awards were concerned with specific spheres of industry. Then, in 1917, the various grades of The Most Excellent Order of the British Empire were introduced, ostensibly to reward service, either meritorious or gallant (or maybe both), in furtherance of the First World War.

Peace having returned almost everywhere in 1918, this order's reason for existence appeared to have vanished, apart from retrospective awards, so its role was extended, but in 1922 the situation was reviewed and the original Medal of the Order of the British Empire was replaced by separate Medals of the British Empire for Gallantry or Meritorious Service. In 1937 the former was redesignated 'The Empire Gallantry Medal' but, notwithstanding the original intention to the contrary, it was also awarded, on occasion, 'in the face of the enemy' and, eventually, was absorbed into the George Cross as were, much later, the Albert and Edward Medals.

Experience at the start of the Second World War, successively in Poland, The Netherlands, France, Denmark, Belgium, Greece and Malta, reflected that during the Spanish Civil War (1936–9) in bringing home the lesson that the need for courage and its expression were not confined to actions in direct contact with the enemy wherever he was encountered.

Most of the relevant experience had been forced upon the civilian population by enemy air attacks, so in 1940, Winston Churchill, the Prime Minister, with his awareness of the importance of maintaining morale in a positive way, ordered that the subject of awards for civilian gallantry under attack be given active consideration. Our armed forces having been expelled from continental Europe it followed that any enemy-initiated conflict in North-West Europe would, for the immediate future, take place on, over or around the United Kingdom.

Tentative proposals for the creation of a Civil Defence Cross together with a Medal had developed into plans for both a George Cross and a George Medal but, after representations from the relevant interested parties, eligibility for these awards was extended. Merchant Navy gallantry and that by the Armed Forces not in active contact with the enemy, i.e. 'actions for which purely military honours are not normally granted' (notably explosive ordnance disposal) were also to be rewarded.

Churchill, in his unforgettable literary style, saw the effect as granting the George Cross for 'outstanding deeds of éclat' and 'George Medals being given in their thousands over the whole area of non-military good conduct and valour'. Whilst, over the years, the result for the Cross has been approximately that anticipated, Medals have not been awarded on such a lavish scale as was expected (see below).

These deliberations resulted in two Royal Warrants being promulgated on 24 September 1940 although they were not published in *London Gazette Supplement* until 31 July 1941 (see Appendix A for that relative to the George Medal). At this stage the amended conditions of the medal awards approved them to civilians and the fighting services for all appropriate acts of bravery in war *and peace*, world wide, for all men and women of or under the protection or jurisdiction of the British Empire (later Commonwealth). The proposal for separate civilian and military divisions was not sanctioned.

A significantly different approach to the subject of gallantry awards was the fact that rank or status were to play no part in awards of the Cross *or* the Medal. This policy applied hitherto to very few British honours and was destined to create confusion for some time in the minds of certain officials of a traditional cast of thought.

It is unlikely that the Australian or Canadian governments will continue to recommend awards of the George Medal since these Realms now have their own honours systems superseding the 'Royal' system. These include full ranges of bravery awards.

Later amendments to the royal warrants described extensions of eligibility; allowed direct submissions to the Monarch by the Dominion governments; reflected political changes in the Commonwealth; altered submission procedures to allow for organisational changes in the Whitehall ministries and, in 1977, an important change, *authorised posthumous awards* (none having so far been granted to women).

With the exception of certain occasions on which the George Medal was used, improperly, to repair deficiencies in the system for granting awards for activities during internal security operations (traditionally known as 'duties in aid of civil power') there is one thread consistently running through actions for which it has been given and that is to *save life* – not take it.

Order of precedence is an essential factor in considering the order of wearing and here the rank/status concept has had its influence. The George Medal was, until 1947, accorded precedence *behind* the King's Police and Fire Service Medal for Gallantry yet the *standard of conduct* was stated to be equal to that for the Distinguished Service Order, the second highest military gallantry decoration for commissioned officers. In 1947 the position was changed to the still anomalous and relatively lowly one immediately *behind* the Distinguished Conduct Medal/Conspicuous Gallantry Medal, the joint second highest gallantry awards for non-commissioned servicemen.

Another significant category of award is the 'honorary' one, that is one given to foreign nationals outside the eligibility parameters of the time. Although approved by the Monarch in the same way as the 'normal' ones, it is not published in *London Gazette Supplement*, the only official medium for public notification in the United Kingdom.* An additional 'standard of conduct' complication was created by the retrospective notification, in January 1946, that foreign nationals could not be awarded the George Cross (breached at least once in the case of an officer holding a British King's Commission under an assumed name) so the George Medal has had to do duty for some acts of gallantry above the standard of that normal to British and Commonwealth winners.

The George Medal has been won by women

– in enemy air-raids in the United Kingdom and elsewhere.
– engaged in underground or Resistance activities in Europe and Malaya.
– in the fight against crime, often involving armed men.

* It is argued that medals, as distinct from orders or decorations, cannot be categorised as 'honorary' but nevertheless these are not normally published in London Gazette Supplement either.

– in other life-saving acts relative to minefields or aircraft crashes.
– in ship attacks by enemy aircraft or submarines.
– in attacks by predators.
– in attacks by deranged men.

In spite of the variety of potentially dangerous situations in which they have been involved, awards to women represent a mere 3.24% of the total, fifty-seven plus nine 'honorary' out of a total of 2,039.

As far as gallantry in air-raids is concerned the omissions are extraordinary since no awards of the George Medal were made to any woman involved in the Clydebank Blitz, the Merseyside Blitz or the heavy air-raids on Belfast, Hull or South Wales.

In accounts of rescue concerning air-raids it is, perhaps, as simple to read the phrase 'buried in rubble' as it would to be record the passing of a shower of rain but, to comprehend fully what it entailed, the following representation of what a typical situation could have involved may help.

> The victim could be encased in rubble containing sharp-edged fragments of brick, tile, stone or concrete mixed with wood, metal or glass, ranging in size from large chunks to near dust, all irregularly shaped. The stability of the whole agglomeration, the component materials of which have come to rest randomly, depends on such imponderables as what parts of the original structure remain in their previous state and the positioning of the furniture, floors, pieces of wood and other detritus. Once the mass has settled down the victim, if conscious, will be aware of choking dust, maybe water or other fluids, increasing coldness or the presence of leaking gas – all, more than likely, in total darkness. As the time passes he* will become increasingly aware of the physical strain imposed by the position into which he* has been forced and the physical pressure being exerted upon him* by the weight of the debris. The victim will also be growing conscious of personal injuries, encroaching numbness/cramp, difficulty in breathing and

* Or 'she'/'her'

his filthy state. In periods of lucidity awareness will extend to strange sounds, particularly with bombing continuing, heavy local traffic moving or when rescue measures are still in train. Another hazard which may be present, outside the victim's perception, could be unseen live electric cables, waiting to be touched. Mankind's oldest and most feared enemy could be approaching – fire! The final and over-riding concern will be that, for all of their efforts, the rescuers will fail to reach the victim in time.

The following chapters deal with awards grouped together, chronologically, under different activities, and an alphabetical list of medals to women is given in Appendix B. Simply to reproduce verbatim copies of individual citations, where they can be obtained, would be a rather sterile exercise so, to give a more rounded picture of each recipient, biographical details, where they are ascertainable, have been included.

Details of the design of the medal and its ribbon are given in Appendix A but the periodic changes of design in the former have been brought about by the change of monarch and, within his or her reign, by changes in the official style, *e.g.* from D:G:BR:OMN:REX: ET INDAE IMP *to* DEI GRA:BRITT:OMN:REX:FID:DEF, or from D:G:BR:OMN:REGINA F:D: *to* DEI GRATIA F.D. on the medal's obverse. The ribbon has remained unaltered since the medal's introduction.

From time to time medals lost or destroyed have been replaced, such replacements being marked with the letter R impressed on the rim near the swivel. Each medal or replacement is named, giving details of the recipient on the rim in large, engraved, serifed capitals.

Chapter 1

Air-raids – London and Suburbs

As far as the Allied land forces were concerned the contrast between the opening months of the First and Second World Wars respectively could not have been more marked. In 1914 the Central Powers (Germany and Austria/Hungary) started to advance in considerable force over foreign soil right from the start and violent, bloody battle involving millions of men was joined within days. Twenty-five years later, Poland having been invaded by Germany and Russia, the protagonists' land forces rushed to their war stations – focused on the Maginot Line – then, Poland having been over-run, settled down to watch each other throughout the severe winter of 1939/40.

This period of seeming inactivity came to be known as the 'Phoney War' and, to some extent, was welcomed as an alternative to the planner's view that 'another world war will mean the end of civilisation'. This theory was linked with fears that aerial bombing would cause tens of thousands of casualties in the UK, overwhelming the available medical services. Then, in late spring 1940, the anticipated German offensive surged through the gap in the Allied defences created by the failure to extend the Maginot Line to the Channel coast, the speed and aggression of the advance causing chaos which culminated in the Dunkirk evacuation.

With British and Allied forces kicked out of continental Europe in June, the German general staff was implementing the initial phases of Operation *Seelöwe* (Sealion), Hitler's plan to invade and subdue the British Isles. The obese, boastful *Reichsmarschall* Herman Göring had given his word, publicly, to the Führer that the 'Royal Air Force would be swept from the skies', thus enabling the invasion to be launched.

An essential element in his grandiose plan was the inclusion of obliterating attacks on radar stations (the full operational value of which he did not completely understand) and fighter airfields in south-east England. These formed a ring to protect London, the seat of government, against assault from the direction of France, Belgium and The Netherlands, all now under German occupation.

As part of the campaign, on Sunday 1 September 1940, a further attack was mounted by the German Air Force (*Lüftwaffe*) on Kenley airfield, an RAF fighter station near Caterham on the outskirts of Croydon, Surrey which had been seriously damaged in previous raids. Bombs fell on the Guards' Depot, then located in Coulsdon Road, Caterham, one exploding in a short road almost opposite the barracks entrance causing casualties among women and children. At the time of the air-raid a cricket match was being played between the Guards' Depot and RAF Kenley and the bomb also caused a number of casualties amongst the players and spectators. **Miss Sonia Vera Carlyle Straw**, an auburn-haired nineteen-year-old part-time air-raid warden, hurried from her home in St. Margaret's Road to the scene where, despite continued bombing, she rendered first aid to a number of the injured and then treated several persons suffering from shock. A considerable time was to elapse before help could arrive so, in the interval, she carried on working entirely alone, exhibiting great courage and resource.

Born at Lowdham, near Nottingham, she was the eldest of four daughters of William Straw, a retired Grenadier Guards sergeant, and had two older brothers. She had attended Caterham Guards' Depot School and was normally employed as a shorthand typist at Messrs. Marshall, Liddle and Dewdney, a firm of solicitors in Croydon. On the evening of 2 October she appeared before the Urban District Council of Caterham and Warlingham where she was congratulated on her award and presented with certificates of proficiency in high explosive and incendiary bomb control.

Wearing ARP uniform she received her George Medal from HM The King at Buckingham Palace on 27 May 1941, her name being one of those which appeared in the first *London Gazette Supplement* to publish the names of winners of the medal. She served later, from April 1943 to July 1945, in the ATS as a clerk in a REME workshop in Kent and married during the war. Mrs Howard now lives quietly in Wimborne, Dorset, her husband having died.

After concentrated air attacks on oil installations at Purfleet, Thames Haven and Shellhaven on the northern (Essex) bank of the River Thames, the Germans launched their first sustained attack on London on the afternoon of Saturday, 7 September 1940. They concentrated their energies further up-river on the London Docks area between Woolwich and Kensington, using a total of 375 bombers in waves, then, except for a two hour break in the evening, continued through the night until 4.30 a.m. On this gloriously sunny afternoon the dock-side boroughs were subjected to the terror of particularly heavy bombing, both high explosive and incendiary, thousands of houses being destroyed.

One of these boroughs was Rotherhithe, stretching from Southwark around the bend of the river to Deptford and south to Bermondsey. Included in this area, running along the river's edge, were the Surrey Docks, the warehouses of which were packed with a wide variety of essential commodities, almost all highly inflammable. To add to these hazards tinder-dry timber, much of it resinous, stacked as high as twenty feet over a vast area, was poised to add to the intensity of fires which, in a very short time, were to burn so savagely that the wooden road blocks then in common use were set alight. To supplement this danger the tremendous vortex of hot air sucked up and distributed burning embers, some a foot long, while dockside cranes buckled in the heat and crashed to the ground, totally destroyed.

Scattered among the docks were streets of working class houses, some even in the shadows of warehouses, and amid this Dantesque inferno on that afternoon, **Miss Grace Rattenbury** was one of the volunteers trying to evacuate the threatened inhabitants to relative safety. Forty years old, educated at St. Paul's Girls School, London and Girton College, Cambridge University, she had been an organiser of the Invalid Children's Aid Association since 1930. Since January 1939 she had also worked, part-time, for the Women's Voluntary Service (now the WRVS) and from the beginning of the war had helped to establish the Citizens' Bureau in Bermondsey Town Hall, Spa Road.

This afternoon she had volunteered to take a WVS van into the danger area on an errand of mercy. The scene was described in a contemporaneous report* as follows:

> There were pepper fires loading the surrounding air heavily with stinging particles so that when the firemen took a deep breath, it felt like breathing fire itself. There were rum fires with torrents of blazing liquid pouring from warehouse doors and barrels exploding like bombs themselves. There was a paint fire, another cascade of white-hot flame . . . a rubber fire gave forth black clouds of smoke so asphyxiating that it could only be fought from a distance . . . There were rats in their hundreds . . .

Setting out through the bombing at 5.30 p.m. she instituted a shuttle service from Sutherland Wharf to a first line Rest and Feeding Centre at Keaton's Road School in Bermondsey. With massive fires threatening to separate people from the mainland and with only one single span bridge from Redriff Road left open she continued driving through the bombing until the last woman and child had been evacuated.

Tongues of flame, bomb craters and an unexploded bomb made the road extremely dangerous but, remaining calm and confident, she carried on without hesitation, steadying everyone by her example. On more than one occasion she had to throw herself to the ground to escape blast from bombs which fell only a few yards away while her van finished its shift with its paintwork blistered and discoloured by encroaching flames. Shortly after this she was transferred to the WVS

* Front Line 1940–1941. (HMSO 1942) pp. 25, 26.

in Chelsea and, on 17 June 1941, she went to an investiture in Buckingham Palace where she received her George Medal from HM The King. Since 1971 she has lived quietly in Cambridge.

Marian Edith Edwards was born at Beckenham, Kent on 5 January 1896, a daughter of a Bank of England engraver, James E. Edwards, whose son was to be killed in the First World War. After attending school at Hamlet Court Road, Westcliff-on-Sea, Marian trained in nursing at Silvertown, east London, and qualified in 1919, taking further certificates in Transvaal, South Africa, and obtaining a certificate of nursing competence at Woolwich Union Infirmary on 11 August 1921, having married Horace Boulton in April 1920.

Qualifying SRN on 17 July 1925 she became a member of the Royal College of Nursing on 6 July 1926 and qualified SCM at the City of London Maternity Hospital on 16 December in the same year. In her subsequent career she widened her expertise by taking courses in housekeeping, store-keeping and supervision of domestics, as well as dietetics. At the City of London Maternity Hospital she became Home Sister and Assistant Matron in 1928 and in 1932 took the post of Matron at Sir Robert Geffrey's Homes, Mottingham Road, Mottingham, south-east London.

Developing another gift of hers, from 1932 onwards she passed various examinations of the Royal Academy of Music, finishing with the qualification LRAM. A gifted pianist and good organist, she was permitted to play the organ in St. Paul's Cathedral. Her only son had been born in 1922 in Johannesburg and eventually served as a regular airman in the RAF.

On the night of 10/11 September 1940 a crude oil bomb fell on the north part of Sir Robert Geffrey's Homes, setting it ablaze. At the time there were only two elderly, bed-ridden patients in this wing, neither of whom, through age or infirmity, had been able to reach the shelter provided for this situation a hundred yards away. The District Warden, having arrived and taken stock of the situation, went away to summon help.

However, **Mrs Marian Edith Boulton** decided that the circumstances were critical enough to act on her own so, without the benefit of a steel helmet or any other form of protection against the continuing bombing and gunfire, she entered the wing which was next to her quarters. The fire was at its height but she managed to reach the ninety-two-year-old patient, a large woman who, completely unaware of the danger that she was in, was refusing to be moved. Nevertheless, Mrs Boulton, herself aged forty-five, hurriedly placed a cover over the old lady then, unaided, dragged her, literally, from the burning building to a place of safety.

On the warden's return, which coincided with the fire brigade's arrival, the Matron was seen to be directing other wardens to remove inmates from another wing, the north wing now being thoroughly alight. Mrs Boulton undoubtedly had saved two patients' lives entirely by her own efforts. Recommended initially for the BEM her award was upgraded to the George Medal with which she was invested by HM The King on 18 July 1941 at Buckingham Palace.

Mr Boulton having died, she married in October 1956 James Murphy, an electrical engineer, retiring to Bexhill-on-Sea, Sussex in the following year. She died at Fonthill, Reigate, Surrey on 15 March 1978 and was cremated at Worth, near Crawley, Sussex.

Further north, on the other side of the Thames, a high explosive bomb fell on the In-Patients' block of the Royal Chest Hospital in City Road, Shoreditch between 3 and 4 a.m. on the morning of 11 September. It destroyed much of the hospital, bursting water and gas mains, fracturing electricity supply cables and covering patients and staff alike with debris.

Thrown into a heap near the door, badly wounded, severely bruised and shocked by the explosion which had destroyed the whole front face of the hospital, Dr Charles André Bathfield, Resident Medical Officer, the Assistant Matron **Miss Catherine Agnes McGovern** (gazetted only as 'Catherine') and **Staff Nurse Miss Patricia Marmion**, who had been talking together in the ground floor boardroom, went to

Miss Catherine A. McGovern ARRC, GM; Dr Charles A. Bathfield GM; Miss Patricia Marmion GM. (photo: Imperial War Museum).

posts. The boardroom had been doing duty as a casualty reception station but they remained at their posts until all patients had been removed from the ruins and sent to another hospital.

Miss McGovern, who was fifty-two years old, had sustained bad cuts about the head, face, neck and body but, although bleeding profusely, refused all help. Glass splinters deeply embedded in a serious thigh wound so impaired her ability to move that she was unable to walk unaided and had to complete her duties, ending with a full round of the hospital, supported by a policeman. Yet at no time did she consider seeking medical help or going off duty, nor would she have accepted this line of argument since the matron was away from the hospital at the time.

Miss Marmion, twenty-four years old and a native of Skibbereen, Co. Cork, was in charge of the men's ward and, after the explosion in which she was badly cut by flying glass, worked her way through the debris until she reached her patients. She succeeded in pacifying them, preventing one, demented by the loss two nights previously of his whole family, from throwing himself to his death through a hole in the wall. She then helped the stretcher parties in their difficult and dangerous task. Another patient, both of whose legs had been broken in a previous air-raid, was pinned in his bed by a dislodged heavy wooden window frame but she freed him and carried him down to the basement on her back.

One more task, ingrained by her training, remained – that of securing the dangerous drugs and removing them to safety – and she completed this vital duty before allowing herself to be evacuated to another hospital. A few days later she was moved to yet another hospital, Grovelands Hospital, Southgate, north London, where she was placed in a bed only for this refuge to be bombed heavily the night after her arrival. In spite of the floor being liberally bestrewn with shattered glass she jumped out of bed with bare feet to help in rescuing other patients and taking them to safety.

Dr Bathfield, a Mauritian, was also awarded the George Medal for his work during and after the bombing; all three recipients were invested with their medals by HM The King at Buckingham Palace on 27 May 1941.

Miss McGovern, who came from King's Court, Co. Cavan, Ireland, returned to the Royal Chest Hospital after her recovery, to be in charge of the outpatients' clinic which had been set up in the ruins, for these were still the days of tuberculosis.

She had trained in St. Giles and Bloomsbury Infirmary, London between 1911 and 1914 and then served as a sister in the British Red Cross Society during the early part of the First World War, landing in France on 6 October 1914. She nursed at Laversine French Hospital, the Allied Forces Base Hospital (No. 7 Red Cross Hospital) and No. 2 Red Cross Hospital before returning to the United Kingdom where she continued to serve in the Red Cross hospital in Kington, Herefordshire. She then nursed in Ampthill Park Hospital, Bedfordshire before leaving the BRCS in November 1915.

While serving at Endsleigh Palace Hospital for Officers, Euston, *London Gazette Supplement* dated 16 February 1920 was published notifying her award of the Royal Red Cross 2nd Class (ARRC) to add to her 1914 Star (Mons Bar), British War Medal and Victory Medal. She had a sister who, during the Second World War, was Matron of the Mile End Hospital and they both returned to the Dublin area of Ireland after many years in the United Kingdom. Nothing further has been heard of them.

Born on 14 March 1916 in Skibbereen, one of three sons and three daughters of a veterinary surgeon, Philip Henry Oliver Marmion and his wife Bridget Sullivan, Patricia started school at Drimoleague National School. Then, between the ages of eight and seventeen, she completed her education at the Convent of Mercy, Skibbereen, following which she trained at St. Nicholas Hospital, Plumstead, south-east London, qualifying SRN on 25 November 1939. She was evacuated to the Southern Hospital, Dartford, Kent at the beginning of September in the following year where she served until transferred to the Royal Chest Hospital.

After she had been discharged from Grovelands she was engaged on loan to the Civil Nursing Reserve and in private nursing before her matron, an ex-QA talked her into joining the QAIMNS(R) in April 1941. She served in Iraq with 28 British General Hospital at Zubaii, Baghdad, spending a period on loan to 28 Combined General Hospital at Mosul. She married an Indian Cavalry officer, Joseph Richard Thorpe, and bore him a son in Quetta, India in October 1944 who is now living in England.

Returning to the United Kingdom she was demobilised in April 1946 and, in a busy career mainly spent in Essex and Middlesex, worked as a staff nurse, nursery matron, school nurse, pupil midwife and health visitor. She married, in March 1954, Tom McKinney, an aircraft engineer, and thus acquired a step-daughter. They returned to the Republic in August 1984 and now live in Donegal, the beautiful county in which her husband was born. Still alert and articulate, an inveterate letter-writer, she now has three grandchildren and has recovered successfully from a hip operation.

The next nurse to win a George Medal, a Welsh woman from Gorslas, north of Llanelli, Glamorgan, was employed on duties outside hospitals. A woman Sanitary Inspector and Health Visitor, **Miss Maria Felicia Thomas**, one of three daughters of Aaron Thomas, a tenant farmer, and his wife Hannah (née George), she was born at Tycroes, Llandeilo Road, Gorslas, Llanelli on 22 October 1903. She attended Penygroes Primary Council School in Llanelli and then trained at Selly Oak Hospital, Birmingham, qualifying SRN in 1927. Over the next eleven years she further qualified as a midwife, health visitor, sanitary inspector and sister tutor.

She was also a nurse in the ARP Casualty Service in charge of a Mobile First Aid Unit (Woolwich No. 1) and, on 7 September 1940, had been called to an incident at 40, Plumstead High Street in south-east London, a coffee shop. These premises had received a direct hit from a high explosive bomb and a man and a woman were trapped under unstable debris supported mainly on forms and tables. After arriving with a doctor she worked her way under the wreckage through a small crawl hole created by a rescue party to administer morphia to the casualties.

In another incident on 20 September, she went to Red Lion Lane, Shooter's Hill at 1 a.m. to find that a high explosive bomb had demolished several cottages, a public house and a shop. Two victims, a man and a woman, were buried for nine hours during which Miss Thomas was to crawl in, again and again, under the debris to administer morphia. Then, after they had been freed from the close embrace of the rubble, she comforted and fed them until they could be released from the mass of debris into the open air.

She was invested with her medal by HM The King at Buckingham Palace on 27 May 1941, having attended a meeting of Woolwich Borough Council on 8 February at which the council congratulated her on the award and recorded their thanks.

After the war she continued to work in Woolwich, where she belonged to the local Welsh Society and sang in the choir, until 1966. In 1967 she returned to Cross Hands, Llanelli to follow her interests of gardening, reading and needlework. A strong but shy personality, thoroughly dedicated to service to others, she died in Singleton Hospital, Swansea on 19 July 1980 and is buried at Penygroes Independent Chapel, Llanelli. Her sister Sarah, who lived with her at Woolwich, was also a nurse, attaining the position of matron, and now lives at Gorslas. Maria Thomas' George Medal was donated to the hospital where she trained, Selly Oak, and is exhibited there.

The apparent paradox in the air-raid situation was that fire brigades depended on the ready supply of a highly inflammable material – petrol – to fuel fire pumps and other equipment used in close proximity to the fires that they were fighting. The continuous nature of the air-raids from 7 September onwards and the effects of further bombs in stoking up the flames meant that those essential appliances could not leave the scene to be refuelled – the need to disconnect, the creation of gaps in the defences and obstruction by collapsed buildings or bomb craters precluded this.

The obvious alternative to taking appliances to the fuel supply was to take the fuel to the working equipment so, in the London Fire Brigade, thirty-hundredweight lorries carried canned petrol to the pumps and other equipment needing replenishment. The LFB was made up of regulars, auxiliary firemen and women auxiliaries, the last generally employed on communications, clerical duties, mobilising ambulances and driving and manning mobile canteens. There was considerable opposition to the employment of women on operational duties although they had been trained in certain aspects of these.

Born on 13 March 1919 at Cambridge Square, Paddington **Miss Gillian Kluane Tanner** was the only child of Mr Selwood Tanner, MC who, after gold prospecting in Alaska and service in the First World War, went to work as racehorse trainer to the King of Egypt. Her parents divorced in 1925 and she was educated in Kensington by a governess, in Farnborough and in Oxford. Joining the Women's Auxiliary Fire Service (WAFS) in the first week of the war, she trained at Tooting before being posted to Dockhead Sub-district. On the

Friday night, 20/21 September 1940, its area of responsibility was under severe bombing attack with six serious fires blazing furiously. It was thus necessary to prevent the appliances dealing with them running out of fuel but there was a shortage of drivers to crew the petrol lorry. Auxiliary Tanner, then twenty-one years old, volunteered to drive it with 150 gallons of petrol in cans on board so, despite continued heavy bombing, she drove from fire to fire in the congested streets of Bermondsey for three hours. She showed remarkable coolness and courage in maintaining the fuel supply to the operational equipment working there.

HM The King presented her with her medal at Buckingham Palace on 17 June 1940. On the formation of the National Fire Service in August 1941 she was transferred to Avery Hill, New Eltham. She was to be the only female member of any fire service to be awarded the George Medal.

Married on 13 January 1945 at St. James, Spanish Place, Paddington to Captain Armitage, DLI, she was demobilised in March of that year and divorced in 1949 with one daughter. Marrying again in 1954, she became Mrs Clark but divorced in 1970 having been engaged in farming and then running a country club. After this she drove a ten-ton lorry for a fell-monger in the Swansea area for ten years, a very noisome occupation. She is now a companion in Lampeter, Dyfed, west Wales.

Part of the medical defence plan against the threat of enemy air-raids was to train doctors and nurses in the techniques required to deal with the resultant heavy casualties. This pool of professional staff would be used to augment the specialist hospitals unable to cope with a sudden influx of patients. During an air-raid on the night of 19/20 November 1940 a high explosive bomb struck B Block of Grove Park Hospital, Mottingham in south-east London and penetrated all three floors. It exploded in a ward on the ground floor where the sole occupant was Miss Gertrude Brawn whose head had been injured in a previous raid. She also had both her legs in plaster and was thus immobilised.

Up to 1940 this hospital had dealt only with tuberculosis patients so a number of the nurses had been posted in from other hospitals. **Miss Ruby Eirlys Megan Rosser**, a twenty-one-year-old staff nurse, who was in the adjoining block, rushed to the patient's bedside and, using her own body, protected Miss Brawn from the serious injury which would have been caused by the rush of debris falling from the ceiling and floor above. She remained at her post as the floor above, together with the equipment from it, continued to fall.

Two other members of staff, **Senior Assistant Nurse Miss Aileen Ruth Turner** and **Staff Nurse Miss Mary Christine Fleming** (only 'Mary' in *London Gazette Supplement*) were involved on the first floor. Miss Turner, the one familiar with the area, led the party to the only place which provided access to the first floor and crawled through a window into a ward where there were four bedridden patients and several others trapped in a corner. When the bomb had struck, hot water pipes burst in this ward, filling the area with steam, and the floor collapsed progressively towards a hole, with beds beginning to slide down the slope.

So, assisted by others, showing coolness and resource, she helped to pass several patients out to safety, shepherding them around a path close to the wall. Miss Fleming, ignoring personal danger, crossed the floor which was giving way rapidly beneath her and led the rescue of the four bed-ridden patients, accomplishing it a few minutes before the whole of the floor collapsed.

Miss Turner and Miss Fleming received their medals from HM The King's hands at Buckingham Palace on 26 September 1941 and Miss Rosser was invested with hers at a similar ceremony on 25 November. Two days later, in the Council Chamber of Llanelli Town Hall, she was given a civic ceremony supported by her grandfather, parents and other relatives.

Miss Rosser was born on New Year's Day 1919 in Llanelli, Carmarthen, the daughter of Ifor Rosser, a journalist on the *Western Mail* and Emily (née Rudall) who also had four sons. She went to Bigyn Girls' School and Llanelli Girls' Grammer School before training at St. Alfage's Hospital, Greenwich (now Greenwich District Hospital) between February 1937 and June 1940 when she qualified SRN. At the time of the bombing she was on loan – a period which was to extend for four months – after which she was to return to her own hospital from where she resigned in 1946 having married Victor Ashdown in March 1944.

She worked part-time in midwifery between February 1947 and 1948, in which year she gave birth to a daughter, and from February to June 1951. Their son having been born in 1952 she started district nursing in December 1958, becoming a Queen's Nurse in January 1962. She left the service in August 1968 to start training as a Health Visitor, qualifying in September of the following year. Until she retired in June 1975 she worked for Greenwich Health Authority and now lives with her husband, a retired local government official, on the edge of Greenwich borough, their lives enriched by four grandchildren.

Miss Fleming was born in December 1916 in Anacarty, Co. Tipperary (now Republic of Ireland), one of nine children, eight of them girls, and was thus twenty-four years old when the incident occurred. Her parents were Michael Fleming, a farmer, and his wife Mary and she went to Ayle National School and Coppawhite Vocational School before training and qualifying in November 1940 at St. Nicholas Hospital, Plumstead.

She nursed on loan to Grove Park, then, after a year, moved to Brook Hospital, Shooter's Hill where she continued until 1955 when she returned to Ireland, nursing at St. Vincent's Hospital, Tipperary until her retirement in 1963. Kind and helpful to everyone, she was five feet six inches tall, a good humoured, caring, most responsible person whose interests were reading and films, playing camogie – the female version of the Irish game of hurling – and badminton. She died on 14 November 1985 in St. Vincent's and is buried in Coppawhite Cemetery.

Miss Turner, who was born in Tunbridge Wells, Kent in September 1919, was a member of the Emergency Hospital Service, having no formal qualification. At the time of her recommendation her address was given as Southborough, a suburb to the north of Tunbridge Wells, but no trace has been found of her since. When the *London Gazette*

Supplement first published her award, her christian name was given as 'Aileen' but an amendment added the second name of 'Ruth'.

Miss Hilda Pauline Hollyer, the daughter of Clive Perring Hollyer and Enid Emily (née Johnstone), was born on 22 December 1907 in Chester, the historic Cheshire city and river port. Her father was a fine art dealer's manager and their marriage had taken place in Chester although the family had originated in south and east Kent, changing its name from Holyer around the end of the eighteenth century.

Before the war she had worked in Windsor and Newton's south Croydon shop as a picture frame maker, joining the ARP Communications Service just after the outbreak of the war. A single daughter, she lived with her parents in Temple Road, South Croydon and was a devout member of the First Church of Christ Scientist, taking part in all of its activities. She was described as short and slim with fair hair, pretty, shy with the gentlest fun-loving temperament, uncomplaining but ready to do anything for anybody.

Darkness in Croydon, as Christmas approached, insinuated itself in late afternoon and was intensified by the silent blackout. In a clear and still evening at 7.40 p.m. on Sunday 24 November 1940, after a glorious day, a single enemy aircraft slipped through the defences protecting south London before the sirens sounded and the guns could open up. In nil visibility two heavy high-explosive bombs were dropped. One of them, weighing 1,000 kilograms, dropped blind, struck Croydon Town Hall where, fortunately, owing to the absence of early warning, there was only a skeleton staff present on duty. The bomb detonated in the basement area (which ran along two sides of the building) on the Fell Road, or east, side exactly opposite the borough police station.

The basement complex contained a drawing office, canteen, VIP shelter and the Southern Report Centre of the ARP Service which the bomb destroyed, bringing down a 25-foot wide slice of the façade and killing three of the five telephonists on duty in the Control Message Room. The other two, Miss Pamela Menzies and Miss 'Wendy'

Pauline Hollyer* (as she was described in *London Gazette Supplement*), who survived, were operating in Main Control Room into which a large heavy window frame was projected by the blast. Miss Menzies, who was sitting in a corner, suffered severe injuries and Miss Hollyer, positioned in the centre of the room, received a wound to the back of her right shoulder.

Four telephones continued to function although buried under debris on the floor and, while Miss Menzies was being evacuated via a tunnel leading under the road to the police station, the main staircase being blocked, these were uncovered. Miss Hollyer, refusing all but the simplest of medical treatment, managed to deal with a ringing telephone before testing all of them to establish which were still working.

She cleared sufficient space to enable her to continue functioning operationally, then, refusing to leave her post unless arrangements could be made for another telephonist to replace her, carried on serving the instruments throughout the evening and night until 8 o'clock next morning. Vital communications were thus maintained without interruption, particularly those relating to the other very serious incident which had occurred when the second bomb fell on the Liberal and Radical Working Men's Club in Scarbrook Road, killing twenty-five people and burying others under the debris.

Dr Oscar Madeley Holden, the fifty-five-year-old Medical Officer of Health and Head of Emergency Medical Services, meanwhile had crawled under unstable, continually shifting debris in the Town Hall basement and, in the extremely confined space available, managed to reach the badly injured in the area of the dead telephonists and administer morphia to the casualties. He also was awarded the George Medal and he and Miss Hollyer received the medals from HM The King at Buckingham Palace on 17 June 1941 after spending a long period recovering from the effects of the bombing.

Two weeks after the bombing Wendy attended her friend Pamela's

* The question of her name is further complicated by the fact that in different documents she is recorded as 'Pauline Hilda' and 'P. J. E.'.

wedding, the photographs of which were destroyed in an air-raid forty-eight hours later. The family moved to Eastbourne, Sussex in 1947 but, tragically, she died at home of cancer on 12 September 1950 at an unusually early age. Her father, who reported the death, was then described, remarkably, as a 'stamp collector'. She is buried in Langney Cemetery, Eastbourne.

Dr Laura Louise Bateman ('Laura' only in *London Gazette Supplement*) was born in Co. Antrim, Northern Ireland in 1903 and qualified MB, BCh, BAO at Belfast University on 28 March 1929. After a period at hospital in Lurgan, Co. Armagh she was awarded a Diploma in Public Health at Birmingham in 1936, then spent a year (1938–9) in the North Eastern Hospital, St. Anne's Road, Tottenham, north London. In 1940 she went to Brook Hospital, Woolwich where she worked as a medical officer with Dr Gerald Edward Breen, a southern Irishman who had qualified in Dublin in 1921.

Brook Hospital (now Brook General) lies on Shooter's Hill Road at the south end of Woolwich Common, south-east London. On the night of Wednesday 29 January 1941, a high explosive bomb fell on the Medical Superintendent's house which it demolished, trapping two housemaids in its ruins. The bomb site was littered with loose wreckage and fallen trees while the hazards to rescue workers already presented by the presence of cellars, a small fire and escaping gas were worsened by the continuing air-raid and falling shell splinters from the intense artillery barrage.

Dr Breen and Dr Bateman both hurried to the scene and a maid was extricated with difficulty in spite of being doubled up in the wreckage, pinned down by a very heavy beam across her shoulders. A faint noise was then detected coming from deep down in the ruins where another maid was buried at the foot of the huge mass of a chimney-breast poised precariously over the devastation. A hospital porter went away to seek some medical equipment and Dr Breen volunteered to crawl in to relieve the maid's suffering by administering an anaesthetic. Dr Bateman however said that, on account of her being much slimmer, her chances of reaching the girl had to be much greater.

So, a small hole having been created, she entered it head first, her ankles being held by another porter. Suspended in this manner she was in constant danger of being crushed should there be a collapse of the large girders, masonry or general debris above and around her, supported as it was only at the ends. Despite this, she succeeded in administering morphia to the maid and did not leave the scene until two hours later, after the girl had been extricated.

Dr Bateman then continued to treat casualties in the operating theatre and wards until the early hours of the following morning; on many previous occasions she had been on the spot working with victims all night and attending to them all day. One of the porters was so impressed with her heroism that he wrote to a daily paper describing her actions. Her recommendation was not initiated until very early in April and so she was not invested by HM The King at Buckingham Palace until 21 October 1941.

Staying at Brook until 1945 she became Resident Medical Officer of the North Eastern, Tottenham until 1947 when she entered into joint practice with Dr Breen in Brook Green, west London. In that year she was shown in the Medical Directory as Administrative Medical Officer in the Ministry of Pension and, in 1948, Deputy Chairman of Medical Services in the Ministry. From the same year she had been assistant editor of the *Medical Press* and she and Dr Breen were married in 1951. Continuing her assistant editorship she lived in Westminster from 1945 to 1958 and now lives in retirement in Lisburn, Co. Antrim, Ulster. Dr Breen died in 1981, a Fellow of the Royal Society of Medicine.

After a two month spell in which enemy aircraft attacked other cities and towns in the United Kingdom, about 150 bombers returned to assault London on each of the nights of 8 and 9 March 1941 – a Saturday and a Sunday – leaving more than two hundred dead each time. Six months after the first catastrophic dockland raids in which lessons in survival had been learned the hard way, the basements of dock buildings in the Wapping area of east London had been taken into use as shelters for the general public. On the first evening **Dr Hannah**

Billig, of Cable Street, Stepney, E1 was going from shelter to shelter attending to the casualties. She was the eldest of two daughters and a son produced by a Russian-Jewish immigrant couple who had settled in London's East End. After a normal schooling she gained admittance to the Royal Free Hospital, London by scholarship, and qualified in 1925 (London University), filling house appointments at the London School of Medicine for Women, the Jewish Maternity Home, the Elizabeth Garrett Anderson Hospital and the South London Hospital for Women. She then set up a general practice in Cable Street, Shadwell, a poor area east of Tower Bridge and on the edge of dockland.

A member of the local Emergency Medical Service, she was medical officer in charge of several air-raid shelters, her qualities of compassion and good communication exercising a calming influence wherever she went. While doing the rounds she was about to get into her car at one point when a high explosive bomb detonated nearby, destroying the vehicle and throwing her violently across the pavement. She ended up at the foot of some stairs with an ankle broken so, to allow her to continue to attend to the casualties in St. John's Shelter in Wapping High Street, her leg was placed in a walking plaster cast. While she was doing this she was called up the street where bombs were still dropping amid tremendous fires, and started administering to the dying and injured, continuing to do so for four hours, totally ignoring the danger. It was early morning before she could be persuaded to go to the hospital for her own injuries to be attended to.

Her courageous actions throughout the London Blitz had already made her well-respected and admired by everybody in the area, but the Regional Commissioner's staff, initially, considered them worthy only of a King's Commendation. This was however, rightly, raised by the Honours Committee to the George Medal with which she was invested by HM The King at Buckingham Palace on 4 November 1941.

When her younger sister qualified, the practice became a joint one and this arrangement continued until 1942 when Hannah joined the Indian Medical Service as a captain and, for outstanding work in Calcutta during the 1944 famine relief, she was awarded the MBE

Miss Hannah Billig GM
(photo: Imperial War Museum).

(Military) in the 1945 New Year's Honours List. She returned to general practice in east London after the war, helping with infant welfare services and taking an active part in the affairs of the local division of the British Medical Association.

She had been a long-serving member of the Stepney Group Hospital Management Committee and the Medical Women's Federation in 1962 before emigrating to Caeserea, Israel in 1964. In a short period she mastered enough of the local language to continue her remarkable work in nearby Arab villages and Jewish settlements until she was well into her eighties. At the end she suffered some years of ill-health and died a much-loved and respected woman on 11 July 1987 with a lifetime of service to humanity behind her.

Chapter 2

Air-raids – South and West

WHILE historical accounts of enemy bombing have given prominence to the 'London Blitz', air attacks in the United Kingdom were by no means confined to the capital. Such attacks were delivered all over the country in pursuance of a number of objectives such as the destruction of ports, industrial areas and communications as well as aerial terrorism, but not all bombs were aimed or dropped as part of the deliberate execution of a plan. Failure to keep to the bombing formation, the understandable desire to jettison and make for home if under attack by defending AA fire and aircraft, or plain inexperience, all played their part and could have resulted in bombs falling well off target. This was made more apparent when such incidents occurred away from major conurbations. The *Lüftwaffe*'s heavy reliance on the master-bombing technique undoubtedly contributed as well.

That is not to say, however, that isolated searchlight or other AA sites were not attacked as constituting lower priority alternative military targets which were better than nothing. Nestling in St. Leonard's Forest, east of Horsham, Sussex, lies the small village of Colegate where, on the evening of 9 September 1940, incendiary bombs were being dropped with the apparent intention of setting light to the forest although they could have been meant for the searchlight site located on the southern edge of the village.

Miss Dorothy May White, who was on duty at the first aid point in the village hall with two other VADs, was born on 19 July 1894 at

Miss D. M. White GM
(photo: Mr J. R. White).

West Lavington, Wiltshire, one of four daughters and one son of Walter White, a gardener, and Eleanor (née Scott). The family moved to Bayworth, near Abingdon, Oxfordshire and she went to school in Sunninghill. From her earliest years she showed a keen interest in the care of babies so, in 1916, she became nurse to the family of Mr and Mrs W. C. Barnes, a teacher and his wife living at Somerton, between Oxford and Banbury.

When Mr Barnes was appointed joint headmaster of Upland House School near Colegate she moved with the family and finally lived with them at Rhododendron Cottage in the village. She was known to everybody as 'Nanny', not only because she was employed as such but also because she was well loved in the village where she could be relied upon for help in any emergency.

After her charges had grown up she joined the British Red Cross Society as a VAD. While she was in the hall one day a high explosive bomb demolished the District Nurse's house next door. The three VADs went to help the nurse, immediately finding her lying head downwards in the crater, alive but badly injured. Under considerable difficulties, they brought her out up the steep, loose side of the hole. Placing her on a stretcher, they took her into the hall where the other two VADs set about treating the nurse's serious head injuries while Miss White went to the other end of the hall to light the primus stove to heat some water.

Another high explosive bomb fell on the hall, demolishing the end where the nurse lay, killing her, fatally injuring Miss Heather Barnes, one of the VADs and injuring the other, Miss Piteathy, in the face and back. Ignoring personal danger Miss White scrambled over the rubble and, finding Miss Barnes (who later died in hospital) terribly injured in the abdomen and leg, applied first aid using a tourniquet made from her belt, all dressings and equipment having been buried by the explosion.

She then manoeuvred the VAD onto a stretcher and, helped by the police, loaded her into an ambulance. Particular poignancy was added to the tragedy of the bombing by the fact that the twenty-year-old

Heather had been one of the five children that she had nursed in the family. After returning to the hall where she found that the nurse's body had been removed she went down the road to help other casualties, attending to one, then finding two others, firemen, dead before dealing with another who died later in hospital. Not content with this, with enemy aircraft dropping delayed-action bombs, she went around all the cottages in the village to check on the situation and give help where it was needed.

Despite the fact that her house had been so badly damaged as to render it uninhabitable she carried on day after day helping the villagers in every possible way, proving to be a tower of strength to all. She was invested with her medal at Buckingham Palace by HM The King on 17 June 1941, it having taken two months after the incident for the recommendation to be initiated.

Other forms of war work in which she was engaged were knitting for the troops and collecting for a National Savings Group and the Spitfire Fund. After the war she continued to nurse the children of earlier charges while remaining active in the BRCS until a fortnight before she died at the Barnes' family home in Osterley, Middlesex in September 1979. She is buried in Colegate village churchyard beside St. Leonard's Church, fifty yards away on the opposite side of the road to the scene in the village hall. Her grave is marked by a simple headstone but she is remembered by all who knew her for her total spirit of service and sense of fun.

A similar set of circumstances occurred on the other side of Sussex when, on the evening of Monday 30 September 1940, with no obvious military target nearby, Buttons Farm near Wadhurst, south-east of Tunbridge Wells, Kent, was struck by three high explosive bombs. One of them killed two women and completely demolished the farmhouse, trapping three children in its ruins. When Mr Edward and Mrs Phoebe Ede and their eighteen-year-old daughter **Miss Rose Ede** arrived on the scene they could hear the children's cries and two girls, aged two and four, were released quickly. The third, a six-month-old baby girl named Heather, remained trapped under the wreckage of an upstairs room and in a bid to rescue her Miss Ede, only five feet two inches tall, crawled under the fallen beams, in danger of being crushed herself at any moment.

With Mr Ede and other neighbours trying to lift the beams she worked to free the baby, moving the infant inch by inch, comforting it all the time, persisting for over half an hour until the relevant beam had been moved sufficiently to enable Heather to be brought out. Throughout the rescue she worked in complete darkness and pouring rain with enemy aircraft overhead, but carried on, wet, filthy and uncomfortable, until the successful completion of the delicate task. She was invested with her George Medal by HM The King at Buckingham Palace on 27 May 1941.

Born in Wadhurst in March 1922, one of a family of three girls and a boy, her parents worked for the farmer but she went into domestic service after leaving school. She married Roy Taylor, a wheelwright, on 13 December 1947 in Lincoln and set up house at Thorpe on the Hill just outside that city but returned to Sussex in April 1982. Her husband died in March 1987 but she has a son and a daughter and lives between Burgess Hill and Lewes in Sussex with one of her daughters.

As part of the campaign to destroy British aircraft factories, forty *Heinkel* He.111 bomber aircraft of the German airfleet *Lüftflotte III* set out with fighter escorts on the afternoon of Monday 30 September 1940 to bomb the Westland Aircraft Company's factory at Yeovil, Somerset. Harassed by RAF fighter aircraft they turned away and finally bombed 'blind' through cloud which was obscuring the area but their loads actually fell a few miles to the east on the town of Sherborne, Dorset. Several hundred bombs struck in a few minutes; thirty houses were destroyed and nearly eight hundred damaged with seventeen people killed and thirty-two more seriously injured. A large proportion of the bombs penetrated roads, causing extensive damage to sewers, surface water drains and utilities including gas, water and electricity. 387 bomb craters were found later as well as several unexploded bombs.

Miss Maude Steele, supervising telephonist of the GPO exchange at the time, refused to leave her post although bombs were falling all around the building and, together with a temporary telephonist, kept the ambulance, fire, police, and ARP and other vital services in constant touch with their respective headquarters. By her courage and sense of duty which was an inspiration to her young colleague she maintained these services until, the majority of the local lines having been put out of action, the exchange became untenable. Destruction even so was such that early calls for outside assistance had to be made by messengers from telephones situated outside the town. After a heavy high explosive bomb had exploded within the Post Office precincts, however, she left the refuge room and went back into the exchange to see if she could be of any service, remaining there until the position became absolutely without hope. Even then she only left reluctantly, having contributed very significantly to the effective and efficient working of all the services for an extended period.

Born in September 1901 she went to the convent school in Sherborne, following this by attendance at Abbey School there and then joined the GPO telephone service in 1916. Promoted to supervisor in 1932 she served in this capacity until 1947 and then married Arthur Davies at Castleton Church, Sherborne in the next year. She had been invested with her medal by HM The King on 27 May 1941. She lived in turn in Woodbridge and Felixstowe in Suffolk, Fremington near Barnstaple in North Devon and New Milton in Hampshire and now lives in retirement in Exmouth, Devon.

Born in Romsey, Hampshire on 22 June 1922 to Edward Archibald Frank Newman, an artist who took up work as a postman as well after the First World War, and Ada Florence (née Cole), **Miss Mary Sybil Joyce Newman** (given as 'Sible' in *London Gazette Supplement*) was a War Reserve Assistant Nurse on Saturday 23 November 1940. With just over a year's service she was employed by the Southampton Medical Services in Hollybrook Home, Winchester Road but, when heavy raiding started, she was off duty visiting her parents at their home in Magnolia Road, Bitterne, an eastern suburb of the city. The attack was made by 121 enemy aircraft dropping 150 tons of high explosive bombs together with 464 incendiary containers.

Between 8 and 9 p.m. a high explosive bomb struck two adjoining houses, 19 and 17 Cypress Avenue, Bitterne, killing outright the four occupants of the former and blowing Mr Hatch out through the doorway of No. 17 into the road where he lay in the debris. After members of the Home Guard had extricated him Miss Newman attended to his injuries and the men started to search the house in the darkness where they found a boy, Albert Hatch, suspended by his ankles, almost upside down, in an extremely agitated state.

Miss Newman transferred her attentions from father to son and, while rescue work was continuing in the presence of gas escaping from a fractured main, comforted and quietened him. To do this she had to enter a hole which had been made in the ruins, in ever-present danger of the debris collapsing, almost succumbing herself several times in the poisoned atmosphere. Despite this she carried on and, after the boy had been extricated and was found to be suffering from severe shock, she obtained hot water bottles and coffee from nearby houses and looked after him until he was removed by ambulance. During the whole period she remained perfectly calm and her efficiency was an inspiration to all – she was still suffering from the effects of coal gas poisoning the following day.

The Regional Commissioner recommended the grant of the George Cross which was changed by the Honours Committee to the George Medal with which she was invested at Buckingham Palace by HM The King on 17 June 1941.

Tragedy struck on her twentieth birthday (22 June 1942) when her father, a senior air-raid warden, was killed in an air-raid. Her mother, with a very young baby, now needed Mary's support more than ever so all ideas of nursing training had to take second place and she remained at Southampton General Hospital until it closed after the war.

To go back in time: she had been christened in Romsey Abbey and attended the Abbey School before the family moved to the Southampton area in 1927/8 where, after attending an infants' school, she finished her education at Middle Road School, Scholing, leaving at the age of fourteen or fifteen. Although her ambition had always been to take up nursing she could not start until her eighteenth birthday so she worked at a number of jobs including one as a nursery maid under a 'nanny' looking after four children. Then, when the ARP (Civil Defence) was formed she became a nursing auxiliary after taking first aid lessons so, reporting to the Royal South Hampshire Hospital, she worked for some months until it was found that she was under age.

After protesting to the local health authority who had required her to leave she was re-assigned to the Hollywood Homes. The children normally accommodated there having been evacuated, the homes were taken into use as an annexe to Southampton General Hospital, dealing with chronically sick patients. These were also moved out after the detonation of a parachute mine blew out the windows so she became a member of the British Red Cross Society, working in an emergency hospital used as a clearing station for air-raid victims and service men and women. After the war, not having pursued her training, she became a registered assistant nurse and took a private post before marrying, on 8 May 1948 at Bishops Waltham, William P. T. Richmond, a butcher in the Merchant Navy, serving on a troopship. They now live in Eastleigh having raised a son and a daughter, and are the proud grandparents of three children. She is still in contact with Albert Hatch.

Miss Dorothy Kate Gardner was born at Northampton on 7 August 1914, three days after Britain declared war on the Central Powers, one of the three children – two girls and a boy – of Reginald Philip Gardner, a gardener, and Kate Ellen (née Smith). She attended school at Cobham Elementary School and started training at the Royal East Sussex Hospital in Hastings. Although living in Milton Heath, Dorking, Surrey she was on duty as a probationary nurse on the night of 7/8 April 1941 when the hospital was bombed. Of medium height, dark and serious with a sense of humour, she was in charge of the private ward which was divided into cubicles where semi-private patients were treated and which, on this night, held three ladies.

When the stomach-churning air-raid alert wailed at 2.20 a.m. she went to the door of the ward and called to the matron to ask whether the patients could be transferred downstairs but, before she could get an answer, heard the whistle of a falling bomb. Without a moment's hesitation, and at the same instant that the bomb struck the balcony immediately outside, she threw herself across Miss Staniforth's bed to protect her. This lady was the occupant of the nearest cubicle and the resultant explosion almost completely destroyed the ward, the roof of which fell in, covering the nurse in an immense amount of debris. Hearing the whistle of the bomb, the matron dashed towards the ward but the explosion took place before she could reach her objective so she called for help and set about removing the debris, helped by two porters who had now reached the scene.

Miss Gardner was released after a quarter of an hour's effort and was found to have sustained very severe injuries – so serious that they were considered as likely to prove fatal; a long wooden splinter had been driven through her skull, the front part of which was missing. Days later it was thought problematical that she should live, her complete recovery being deemed unlikely. Owing to the nurse's self-sacrificing action Miss Staniforth had suffered only bruises to a shoulder. However, on 21 October 1941, Miss Gardner was able to receive her medal at the hand of HM The King at Buckingham Palace.

She qualified in 1946, having taken a long time to recover from her horrendous injuries, then, in 1949, she started to train at the Church Missionary Society's school at 'Foxbury', Chislehurst, Kent, continuing at St. Michael's College, Oxford and then completing her studies with the Church Army. Sent to the Telegu speaking area of India in what is now known as Andhra Pradesh she was unable to master the difficult language completely and returned to England in 1957. A five year period of geriatric nursing preceded posts as matron at Christ College, Brecon, mid-Wales and Lancing College, Sussex. She then took up a post in the Cardiff branch of the National Blood Transfusion Service, retiring finally in 1970, and now lives quietly in West Wittering, near Winchester.

As part and parcel of their determination to starve Britain into submission the enemy regarded Bristol, a major west-coast port vital to the established import lifeline, as a legitimate target. So on the night of 16/17 March 1941, with a raid by 162 enemy aircraft in progress, a request for help was received at Bristol Maternity Hospital in Southwell Street off St. Michael's Hill. The message was to say that a woman, believed at the time to be about to give birth, was trapped under debris at a house nearby so **Miss Elsie Lilian Stevens**, a thirty-two-year-old assistant matron, and **Miss Violet Eva Alice Frampton**, a thirty-one-year-old nurse, volunteered to go to her assistance. Making their way through an area made more dangerous by falling aircraft bombs and masonry, having to pick their way through shattered glass, they arrived at the house to find, in fact, that six people were trapped in a cellar in conditions so hazardous that the rescue squad considered that to begin reasonably safe rescue operations would be impossible.

Access into the wreckage was perceived to be through an 18 inch wide grating so the two midwives were lowered, feet first, by this route but then found it necessary to lie flat in order to reach one patient. Although it was not known at the time, one man and one child were already dead, the other four victims being completely trapped. The only light available was that from a torch but, together with the rescue party, the two midwives succeeded in releasing two children and their grandmother who were given stimulants and passed up through the grating to safety. At this stage Miss Frampton returned to the hospital to obtain a supply of morphine then, arriving back at the scene, found that Miss Stevens, crawling over the head of a bed, had located the pregnant woman buried entirely in a tangle of beams under debris. Cutting away part of her coat, the only thing visible, the woman was given a morphine injection but, with continuing detonations, overhead rescue operations had to be abandoned. Ignoring these conditions and their fear that rats were present in the debris the two ladies carried on in the choking dust and escaping gas and, at 3 a.m., freed the victim's head and were thus able to make her more comfortable, sustaining her with sips of tea.

Eventually, at 7.45 a.m., they summoned a woman doctor who stayed with them until they were released at 1 p.m., the victim being taken straight to hospital. Her life, and that of her child that she successfully bore, had been saved by the midwives' bravery and devotion to duty. Both of them were invested with the George Medal by HM The King at Buckingham Palace on 7 October 1941.

Born at Barry, Glamorgan on 24 November 1908, Miss Stevens was one of three daughters of Mr W. J. Stevens, a railway inspector who also had a son. Educated at High Street Schools and Barry County Girls' School she achieved a long-standing ambition when she started general nursing training at Southampton Borough Hospital. She then joined Bristol Maternity Hospital in 1938 where she completed her midwifery training after short periods at Moreton-in-Marsh, Gloucestershire and Llandough, Cardiff Hospitals.

In 1942 she moved to the Shrubbery Nursing Home, High Wycombe, Buckinghamshire and in February was married to Francis Thomas Rice at Paddington Registry Office. Moving to Jersey, Channel Islands, she joined Jersey Maternity Hospital as night sister, becoming matron in 1969, her husband having died in November 1964. She retired in December 1975 and returned to Barry where she now lives with one of her sisters.

Miss Frampton (known throughout her working life and retirement as 'Frampy') was born in 1909 at Ryde, Isle of Wight, the youngest of two daughters and two sons of a head gardener, and went to school at Bettesworth Road School. She completed her nursing training at Shepton Mallet then her midwifery training before nursing at Bath and Bristol. From Bristol Maternity Hospital she went to the Shrubbery in 1941 and became assistant matron in 1961 and matron in 1965. A tireless worker, excellent nurse and a truly professional midwife, she was a born organiser who combined a constant demand for perfection with a sense of humour and her sometimes formidable manner did not conceal her devotion to her staff and above all to her patients. An excellent cook, she used her gift to contribute to the variety of activities that she gave to church and community. She died firm in her Christian faith at High Wycombe on 31 December 1981 and was cremated at Amersham, Buckinghamshire.

The second daughter of Arthur Stuart McNairn who, with his wife, had been a missionary in Peru, **Alison Jean McNairn** was born on 21 May 1912 at Twickenham, Middlesex. Soon after her birth she was taken to live in north London then, at the age of nine, her father moved to Edinburgh where she attended Edinburgh Ladies' College (since renamed 'Mary Erskine School for Girls') for three years before returning to London and studying at a secondary school in Streatham. She qualified MB, BS at the London School of Medicine for Women, Royal Free Hospital in 1936 and then filled a number of house appointments, medical, surgical, obstetric and gynaecological, including those at Bolton and Manchester.

In 1939 Dr McNairn had taken up an Obstetrics and Gynaecological post in the City General Hospital in Greenbank Road, Plymouth, Devon (an old borough hospital) now rebuilt as Freedom Fields Hospital. The city and its adjoining dockyard base of Devonport were subjected to frequent bombing so much that, eventually, the centre of the city was almost totally destroyed. In air-raids on the nights of 20 and 21 March 1941 a total of 293 enemy aircraft flew over the city, dropping 346 tons of high explosive bombs as well as 1,884 incendiary containers. Her hospital was hit at about 7 p.m. on the first night by a stick of five high explosive bombs, one of which buried her in debris up to her neck with two broken ribs, bruising and a damaged foot.

She had been reassuring the mother of a newly-admitted patient in the children's ward which had suffered most damage and which, in addition to sick children, provided shelter for a number of babies and toddlers who had been taken into care. Immobilised as she was, she had to warn rescuers not to walk all over her as they strove to reach those casualties that they could see in the poor light. Despite her injuries and the effects of shock, once she had been released, she went into the area in which she could see that children were being laid out in a row and then spent the rest of the evening establishing which were still alive. These she carried, one at a time, to the adjoining maternity wing where they were put into beds beside the patients already tucked up there, these children remaining there, comforted, until their needs could be attended to.

She also gave assistance to a woman in labour, then dealt with injured patients brought from other hospital wards and certain air-raid casualties which had been admitted from outside. Dr McNairn did not consent to having her own injuries dealt with until surgical operations were again in progress in the hospital and the pressure of duties was lessening. Despite having been on duty since 8 a.m. on the 20th she continued to work although suffering considerable pain which persisted even after she had been treated, and did not go to bed until 6 a.m. next morning, at the end of a period of duty extending over twenty-two hours. Afterwards, in spite of her injuries, she returned to her duties without taking any time off – the very thought of which she has since described to the author as 'ridiculous!'. Her medal was presented to her by HM The King at an investiture in Buckingham Palace held on 4 November 1941.

At the end of 1942 she was commissioned into the RAMC and, during her military service which included treating ATS and military families in Bovington Camp, Dorset and Catterick Camp, Yorkshire, she became interested in the psychological aspects of her specialisation.

Released from the Army with the rank of major in 1946, she went to the Maudsley Hospital at Denmark Hill, south-east London for six months which she extended by three years, qualifying DPM. Here she met Dr John Garrett Jesson and they were married in June 1949 at the Parish Church of St. Mary, Addington, Surrey, both of them then practising at Bethlem Royal Hospital. In December 1949 they moved to Virginia Water, Surrey, then, her elder daughter and son having been born, the family left, in October 1953, for Wickham, near Southampton where her other daughter was born.

When her children were receiving full-time education she began work part-time at the local psychiatric hospital then extended this to full-time work after they had all left home. Her husband, who had been

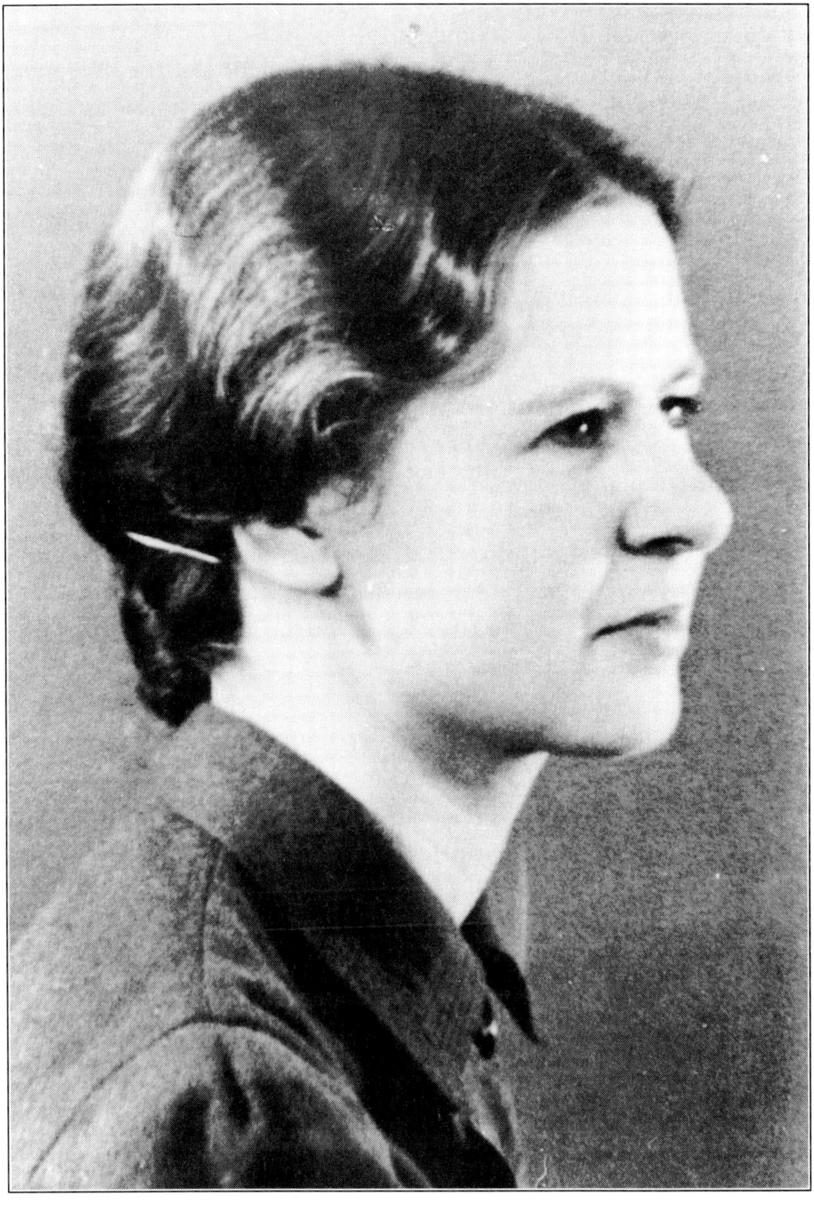

Dr Alison J. McNairn GM
(photo: Mrs Alison Jesson).

a Far East prisoner of war in camps in Korea during the Second World War, died very suddenly in 1976 and a year later she had to retire, having reached the age limit. She now lives quietly in Rotherham, Yorkshire near her elder daughter.

Further air-raids on Plymouth on the 28th and 29th of the following month, in which 286 aircraft saturated the city with 369 tons of high explosive bombs and mines and 1,351 containers of incendiaries, gave rise to another award, this time on the streets around Fort Austin Avenue, Crownhill, a north-eastern suburb. On the second night, when a parachute mine detonated devastating the area, the ambulance driven by forty-five-year-old **Mrs Mary Ellen Fitzgerald** ('Mary' only in *London Gazette Supplement*) was despatched to the scene but a number of bombs fell after she arrived, a near miss wrecking the whole of the coachwork and the vehicle frame-work on top of her. Scrambling out of the wreck Mrs Fitzgerald succeeded in extricating her attendant, taking the badly shocked and semi-hysterical girl back to the ambulance post.

On arrival Mrs Fitzgerald asked for another vehicle to drive, then, having been allocated a replacement, drove it to Fort Austin Avenue where she loaded up with casualties and took them to the Royal Naval Hospital at the west end of Union Street which itself had been badly damaged. She carried on with this duty throughout the whole of the rest of the raid. After the 'All Clear' had sounded its loud continuous message of hope, she drove back to the scene of the original incident from where, its engine being sound and too valuable to discard, she took the ambulance in. To complete the night's work she went to the top of Maradon Hill and brought back another damaged ambulance. The second woman in Plymouth to win the George Medal, she was invested with it by HM The King at Buckingham Palace on 22 December 1941.

She was born at Littleham, Exmouth, Devon on 5 June 1892, a daughter of Patrick Lane, a commissioned boatman of HM Coast-guard, and Catherine Mary (née Power). She went to school locally and, on 2 January 1914, was married at the Roman Catholic Church of the Holy Cross to David Patrick Fitzgerald, son of another commissioned boatman and a Petty Officer First Class in the Royal Navy, serving on the 18,600 ton battleship HMS *Bellerophon*. Widowed on 6 October 1922, her husband having contracted tuberculosis during service on destroyers, she was left to bring up two sons.

At the start of the Second World War while living at Widney Lodge, Crownhill she became an ambulance driver. On the same morning that she was officially notified of her award she was told that her mother had died. After the war had ended, with a war-time colleague, she ran the Dewi Sant Guest House in Eggbuckland Road, Efford then, in 1964, she retired to Yelverton, nine miles north of Plymouth, having suffered a breakdown. Towards the end of her life she entered St. Peter's Convent at Plympton St. Maurice where she died on 26 January 1973 and is buried in Plymouth Old Cemetery, Ford Park Road.

The regular packet services between Ireland and the United Kingdom continued to run during the war and, at 1 a.m. on Friday 13 June 1941 (an unlucky day according to generations of mariners), the 1,922 ton SS *St. Patrick* sailed from Rosslare, Co. Wexford, heading for her home port of Fishguard, Pembrokeshire on a voyage of over sixty miles. The ship had been built in 1930; it was owned by Fishguard and Rosslare Railways and Harbours Co. and commanded by Capt. J. Faraday. There were ninety people, twenty-four of whom were passengers, on board, including the master's young son, as they steamed eastwards at 19 knots across the moonlit Irish Sea.

Nearer to their destination a *Heinkel* floatplane (He.115) was waiting, secured to a buoy, but it was disturbed by the Royal Navy destroyer HMS *Wolsely* which was on convoy escort duties. The float plane took off and sighted the packet steaming independently. Shortly before dawn, at 2.15 a.m., in position 50°04'N, 5°25'W, 15 miles from Strumble Head, west of Fishguard Bay, it came in low, dropped four high explosive bombs and attacked her with machine gun fire. The bombs struck the bridge and penetrated to the fuel tank below setting the ship on fire at once and, in less then four minutes, with her bridge obscured by flames, she broke her back and sank. At very considerable risk to his life the Chief Radio Officer succeeded in transmitting a distress call and the Second Engineer managed to save three of the engine-room staff and a wounded army officer.

Miss Mary Elizabeth Owen was born in May 1898 at Duffryn, Goodwick, near Fishguard, the eldest of William Thomas Owen's five daughters, all of whom like him lived into their seventies. His career was rather out of the ordinary – shipwrecked as a Merchant Navy apprentice while rounding Cape Horn he survived on a remote island by eating goat and sheep meat before being picked up. Later he was employed by the GWR at Fishguard Harbour and for many years served as coxswain of the Fishguard lifeboat, dying in 1945. Mary Owen was educated at Henna School near Goodwick after which she worked as a children's nurse and a general companion before going to sea on *St. Patrick* in 1937.

Known popularly as 'May', she had previously looked after the captain's son on shore as a children's nurse. On the voyage from Rosslare she was the steerage stewardess and, as such, her responsibility lay with the woman passengers on the lower deck. Imbued with overwhelming sense of duty, the lighting system having been destroyed, she felt her way through the darkness from the after-cabin down to the women's berths on the lowest deck. Here she found the doors jammed so tightly that she could not open them by normal means but abandoning the scene would have meant leaving them inside to a horrible death by drowning so she renewed her attack on the doors and, by a supreme effort, struggling with all her strength, succeeded in forcing them open.

Urging the five women that she found inside to move quickly, she accompanied them up to the welldeck where, having been given a life-belt each, they were placed in a lifeboat. At this stage, lacking a life-belt herself, she remembered that a girl passenger was still below so she returned there and brought the terrified girl to the deck. Holding onto her, she jumped overboard. Clinging desperately to the

Miss Elizabeth May Owen GM, Lloyds War Medal (photo: The County Echo*).*

girl, Miss Owen swam and trod water for two hours, encouraging others in the water not to give in. She was eventually picked up by a whaler from HMS *Wolsely*, together with a nurse passenger whom she had been supporting. Seventeen of the crew, one gunner and twelve passengers had been lost but the destroyer and an armed trawler, HMS *Indian Star*, rescued sixty survivors between them and landed them safely on the 14th.

On their way to shore the destroyer's company looked after the survivors, cleaning oil from them, cooking and washing clothing, drying, ironing and even providing emergency clothing.

Miss Owen was presented with her medal at an investiture by HM The King at Buckingham Palace on 21 October 1941. The ship's Radio Officer, Norman William Campbell, and the second Engineer, Francis Joseph Purcell, were each awarded the MBE (Civil) for their actions and all three were awarded the Lloyd's War Medal for Bravery at Sea, Miss Owen being the first woman to receive this medal. She still remains the only woman to be awarded both that and the George Medal.

After the disaster she decided to stay ashore and was employed as a switchboard operator in the Railway Telegraph Office at the harbour until she went back to sea in 1955. This was the year in which she married Victor Pearce, a widower who was a general assistant at the harbour helping customs officers examine cargo. She retired in 1960 and went to live in their home Swn y Mor (Sound of the Sea), Hoel Feidr Dylan, Goodwick where she died in 1972. She is buried in the cemetery in Llanwnda, on the west coast of Fishguard Bay, her medals passing to her youngest sister who presented them on 4 June 1982 to the Sealink office at Fishguard Harbour where they are displayed in the Conference Room.

Well into the third year of the war, with the Allies mounting increasingly effective attacks on German cities, Hitler ordered that 'the air war against England [sic] is to be given a more aggressive stamp. Accordingly, when targets are being selected, preference is to be given to those where attacks are likely to have the greatest possible effect on civilian life . . . terror attacks of a retaliatory nature are to be carried out against towns other than London.' Because of the widespread nature of these attacks they came to be associated with an internationally known series of guidebooks and were thus labelled 'Baedeker' raids. The series started with several attacks on the city of Exeter, Devon and an innovation was the introduction of a new incendiary bombing technique which produced unprecedentedly high concentrations of such bombs on the target.

The third and heaviest attack on Exeter took place on the night of 3/4 May 1942 and the City Hospital at Heavitree (now reconstructed as the Royal Devon and Exeter Hospital) was particularly badly hit, big fires breaking out. The thirty-nine-year-old permanent night duty nurse on the male sick wards in A block was **Mrs Emily Alberta Marden Knee** who had been born in 1902 in Exeter where she subsequently went to school. One of a family of three boys and five girls whose father was Albert George Pearce, she trained as a nurse in Portsmouth before marrying William Knee, a soldier in the Royal Army Medical Corps, in 1923.

With two male nurses she was at her duty station in the middle of three floors where she was responsible for thirty-three patients, twenty-two of whom were elderly and bed-ridden. The air-raid alarm sounded at 1.40 p.m. and shortly afterwards, while she was using the stairs, incendiary bombs penetrated the roof of the upper flight landing, coming to rest, alight, on the stairs, so she dashed to the ground floor and reported the situation.

Then, with one of the male nurses, she went upwards to her own ward, past the bombs on the now burning stair-treads, continuing onto the top ward where ten fires could be seen involving some of the beds and patches of floor; most of the patients had already left their beds so she got the others, two of whom were blind, off the floor and downstairs to safety. This accomplished, she and the male nurse started to fight the fires with sandbags, stirrup pumps and a chemical fire extinguisher, trying to prevent the blaze reaching the first floor but without success. Making arrangements for the ground floor to be evacuated, she started moving the first floor patients next, dragging some of them on their mattresses along the floor to the stairs where help was available.

As she was working on the last mattress the roof at the far end started to collapse and she was dealing with the remaining bed-ridden patients when beds, falling through the ceiling above, cut her off with two patients at one end while six completely bed-ridden men were stranded in the middle of the ward. A member of the NFS unit then insisted that she leave before the central stairs collapsed and, immediately after she had complied and got out three helpless men from the ground floor into the garden, the roof and stairs plunged down in a roar of flame.

A witness of the scene described it later as 'lighted up like broad daylight' and Mrs Knee as 'exhausted doing two men's work, groping about . . . could just be seen in the smoke-filled ward where the heat was unbearable.' In his opinion she got out only just in time to save herself. Mrs Knee received her medal at an investiture at Buckingham Palace on 10 November 1942. Two BEMs (Civil) were awarded to other women and Commendations to four men and three women for activities in the hospital during the attack.

After Heavitree she worked in the School Health and Public Health Clinics until September 1951 when she emigrated to Cambridge, Ontario, Canada with her husband and younger daughter who by then had trained and qualified as a nurse at Princess Elizabeth's Orthopaedic Hospital. In Cambridge she joined her elder daughter who, marrying a Canadian, had accompanied him on his return home after the war. Mrs Knee started work in Galt Hospital in December 1951, transferring later to South Waterloo Memorial Hospital (now Cambridge Memorial Hospital) and retiring because of ill-health in 1966, her husband having died in 1964. She lives now in a senior citizens' home where she does her own housework and cooking, sustained by the thought that all her nine grandchildren and fourteen great-grandchildren are living nearby.

Chapter 3

Air-raids – Scotland and the English Midlands

DURING the war Scotland was subjected to a variety of air attacks extending from hit-and-run bomber attacks to the 'Clydebank Blitz' but only two George Medals were awarded to women for air-raid gallantry and these incidents were not on Clydeside.

The first was on the east coast at Montrose Royal Asylum in Angus where, at 7.30 a.m. on Wednesday 2 October 1940, the unmistakable drone of enemy bombers' engines out to sea was followed by a stick of five high explosive bombs falling in the asylum ground. These were a mile away from the RAF airfield, undoubtedly the true target. One of the bombs struck the edge of the kitchen roof in the female block in which eighty-two, mostly elderly, mental patients were accommodated, demolishing part of the kitchen and blowing in all the surrounding windows. Four female patients were injured by flying glass, steam and water escaped from damaged pipes and, after the first two or three minutes, all the lights failed, plunging the block into darkness.

Two of the staff, **Miss Violet Eleanor Reid**, a twenty-seven-year-old junior nurse, and a colleague, Nurse Simpson, were working in the kitchen at the time and the latter fell to the floor seriously injured. Violet Reid, despite cuts and bruises to face, body, hands and legs, loss of blood and being deafened by the noise of the explosion, remained calm in the intense darkness, attending to the frantic patients as they gathered around her, excited and confused. This done, she returned to her colleague and carried her unaided upstairs to bed where she attended her until a doctor arrived to take over.

Returning to the patients who, by now, had gathered in the entrance hall, mostly in night attire with hysteria only just suppressed, this quiet, shy woman quickly regained control over them by sheer force of personality. When the assistant matron arrived Miss Reid had obtained warm coats and was helping the patients into them, refusing help for herself until she was finished.

Only then could she be persuaded to walk to the first aid post, her cool and cheerful conduct having successfully prevented confusion from developing into widespread blind panic. After many weeks in hospital she was fit enough to attend an investiture at Buckingham Palace to receive her medal from HM The King on 27 May 1941. Even after a period of taking things easy she was unable to continue nursing because, in her own phrase, 'her nerves went to pieces'.

Born on 15 May 1913 in Arbroath, Angus she lost her mother at the age of three and went to live in Essex where she was educated at Holmewood College, Westcliffe-on-Sea until she returned to her birthplace in 1929. Her father, David Reid, was the manager of Alexander Shanks & Sons, manufacturing engineers whose name had been familiar for years on lavatory ware. For three years she worked as a children's nurse in Newport-on-Tay, Fife then started training as probationer nurse in the asylum in 1937 and had become engaged to Patrick Leahy, a regular airman in the RAF. At the time of the bombing incident he was serving in Iraq and they were married in 1942.

The second child, she was the eldest of three daughters, one of whom was a nurse in Edinburgh. Her two brothers were serving at sea, one in the Royal Navy and the other a merchant seaman. Her home was at Wynona Cottage, Cairnie Lane, Arbroath but after her marriage she accompanied Patrick on service to Leeds, Church Fenton (Yorkshire), London, Arbroath and Glasgow. Retiring from the RAF as a flight sergeant, he worked in the engineering division of BEA/BA until his final retirement, dying in 1978. Mrs Leahy still possesses a lively sense of humour and three sons, and lives in Clarkeston, Glasgow.

Many prime bombing targets were to be found in the Midlands – aircraft factories, light and heavy engineering and chemical works among them in Coventry together with important, even vital, junctions in road, rail and canal systems, these having been visited regularly by the *Lüftwaffe*. Intermingled with these were houses, shops and public facilities but saturation bombing did not differentiate between these even had it been thought necessary by the enemy to do so. On the night of 19 October 1940 **Miss Betty Amelia Quinn** ('Betty' only in *London Gazette Supplement*), a seventeen-year-old cadet corporal in the St. John's Ambulance Brigade, was rendering voluntary service at ARP Post No. 300A in Hen Lane School, Rowley Green, north-east Coventry, her home being a short distance away in Dymond Road.

Born in George Street, Coventry on 19 July 1923 she had been at Holbrook Lane School and Barrs Hill Secondary Grammar before joining the SJAB Nursing Cadet Division. She obtained employment first as a stores clerk in Dunlop Rim and Wheel Co. at Holbrook's and then as assistant nurse in the surgery. On 21 September 1939 (less than three weeks after war had been declared) she joined the ARP in a temporary capacity. Her father, Edwin Quinn, was a service engineer in the Riley Motor Works in Coventry, she being the eldest of the two girls and two boys in the family.

On the Saturday night a shower of incendiaries fell on the district and her reaction, without waiting for assistance, was to run outside to deal with a number of them unaided, ignoring shell splinters from the anti-aircraft barrage falling all around. High explosive bombs then started falling and she helped an injured man to a private shelter. After this, despite bombs continuing to rain down, when a report was received of an Anderson shelter (a small corrugated structure, partly buried in gardens, for family use) in the garden of a house in Dymond Road having suffered a direct hit by a high explosive bomb, she ran to the scene and started digging in the crater.

With other rescuers now arriving by the minute she stayed to help dig out several survivors and then attended their injuries until they were removed by ambulance, although shells were still exploding overhead. After handing over her casualties to professional medical personnel she returned to the post where she continued to treat distressed people, giving them comfort. On 27 May 1941 she attended an investiture at Buckingham Palace where she received her medal from HM The King, the first member of the SJAB and the second youngest girl to be awarded the George Medal.

As a result of the publicity at the time of the investiture a photograph of her was taken outside the Palace and reproduced in the *Rhodesia Herald* and the cutting was sent by the Popkiss family living in Southern Rhodesia to their son studying at a dental college in Edinburgh. He forwarded this to Betty to show how far afield her story had been disseminated and the upshot was that, on 21 November 1942, at Holy Trinity Church in Coventry, they were married.

When the 12,000 ton cargo-passenger steamer *The Sydney Star* left Liverpool on 12 February 1943, among the passengers on board were Mr and Mrs Edward Popkiss, who spent the next month zig-zagging, un-convoyed, on passage to Cape Town, South Africa, arriving there on 14 March. Three days later their train reached Salisbury, Southern Rhodesia where he joined the Rhodesian Army and was seconded to the RAF as a dental officer. Betty Popkiss spent a year teaching at St. Peter's School, Bulawayo before giving birth, in June 1945, to her first son who is now Cape Town's Medical Officer of Health.

Her daughter, who qualified later as a nurse in Bulawayo, was born in 1950, three years after Betty's parents, having emigrated, settled in Salisbury. Her younger son was born in October 1959 and, working in a bank, is now reading for a degree. After practising in Bulawayo Mr Popkiss moved to Knysna on the Cape Province coast in South Africa in 1967 where his wife worked in his surgery for three years until, in 1975, they went to live in Cape Town where they still have their home. Betty's life is now filled with her husband, children, grandchildren and animals, all of whom she says keep her fit and happy.

To call the tactic which destroyed or damaged more than half of the city's houses and factories 'saturation bombing' was to understate the horrifying attack experienced by Coventry on the night of 14/15 November 1940. It introduced a devastating new technique which came to be known as 'coventration', a word considered to be of such supreme significance that it was absorbed into the German language. Guided by the *Knickebein* radio navigation beam guidance system all the way from their bases in Bavaria and elsewhere on the continent, 449 bombers struck in full moonlight. On a clear, cold, frosty night just after 7 p.m. parachute flares were followed by incendiaries incorporating explosive charges, then parachute mines and high explosive bombs. Before the attack finished at 6 a.m. next morning, 880 incendiary canisters together with more than 500 tons of high explosive had been dropped, killing more than 550 people and injuring 900 and totally disrupting the telephone and public utilities while the public transport system was all but wiped out.

This was the raid that saw the original Coventry Cathedral reduced to a smoking heap of ruins while, in addition to twenty-one factories – the ostensible targets – two hospitals were badly hit. **Miss Marjorie Eileen Perkins**, a twenty-five-year-old works nurse in Messrs Pattison and Hobourn Ltd's weaving factory in Cash's Lane, spanning the canal at Foleshill, was in charge of the works surgery and should have gone off duty at 10 p.m. However, owing to the heavy and sustained attack she remained until 9 a.m. next morning and, during the whole period, rendered excellent service to casualties in the works, in nearby streets and at the public shelter at Messrs O'Brien's office, a short distance away. During all this period bombs continued to fall and, on two occasions, blast threw her across the surgery, the first causing internal injuries and the second knocking her unconscious.

Recovering consciousness, although in very great pain, she carried out her ministrations, dealing with all casualties in the works as well as outside, inspiring and tending those work people who could not be moved, visiting shelters, encouraging everybody to remain calm. She worked throughout the night with no regard for personal safety under

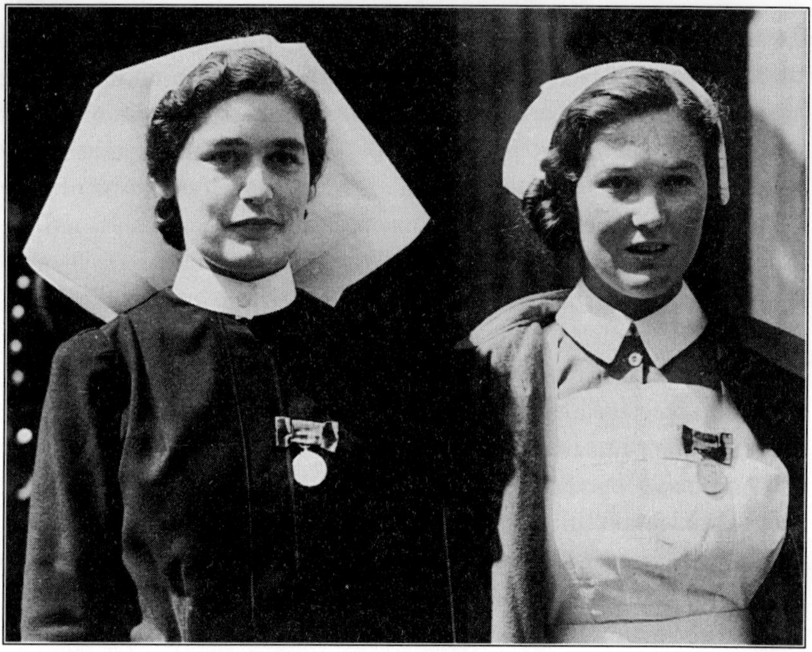

Miss Marjorie Perkins GM; Miss Mary S. J. Newman GM (see chapter 2) (photo: Imperial War Museum).

the most trying circumstances but, on going off duty, had to remain under her doctor's care in her own house in Norman Place for six weeks until after Christmas. She received her medal at an investiture on 17 June 1941 at Buckingham Palace, one of eight ladies on that occasion to receive the George Medal from HM The King.

Marjorie Perkins first saw the light of day in Coventry on 27 March 1915, the daughter of John Perkins, a master mechanic in the Alvis Motor Co., and his wife Amy (née Newey). She went to public and high schools in Coventry, then started nursing training at the Coventry and Warwickshire Hospital but left in 1939 after a year to become a works nurse. In the early part of the war she enrolled as a full-time nurse in the first aid point in Livingstone Road, Foleshill, then was employed at Messrs Pattison and Hobourn from 1939 to

1945. In September 1941, at Holy Trinity Church, she married Herbert John Harris, the church organist at St. John Bablake Church, Coronation Street and gave birth to a son in January 1943 and a daughter in May 1953.

Her husband had been elected FRCO in 1933 and had previously officiated as organist at the Methodist Church as well as at St. Mark's Church. During the war he was absent on service with the RAF. In December 1954, they emigrated to Canada where, from 1955 to 1958, John Harris was organist at St. Paul's Anglican Church, Charlottetown, Prince Edward Island. They moved to Orillia, Ontario in 1963 but her husband died at the end of the following March. She married again in July 1966 to Charles Jackson, a welder and motor mechanic who retired in 1976. By this marriage she added a step-son to her family and now has five grandchildren and two great-grandchildren. She returned to nursing and, from 1964 to 1976, worked as an occupational health nurse for a firm in Orillia for which, at the age of seventy-five, she is still employed as a relief nurse.

With its industries of machinery and tools, foundries and smelting, the town of West Bromwich, bounded by Birmingham, Walsall and Swethwick, was attacked on the night of 19/20 November 1940, the initial assault being carried out by means of incendiary bombs. **Miss Charity Bick** of Maud Road was a bicycle despatch rider attached to ARP Wardens' Post B 13 at Sam's Lane, West Bromwich, having gone there when the alarm sounded. Her father, William Albert Bick (works engineer at a small iron works), was the post warden and when, shortly after the alarm had sounded, incendiaries began to land on the roofs of the surrounding houses, she helped him to extinguish them using a stirrup pump – a small device used to propel a low pressure jet of water from a bucket. During these activities they saw a bomb land on the roof of a nearby pawnbroker's shop to which they gained access and went up to the bedroom, taking with them the occupier's pump and a bucket of water.

The pump, however, would not work – a not uncommon state of affairs after a long period of disuse – so, climbing into the false roof where the bomb had lodged and was now burning on a ceiling joist, they extinguished it by splashing water with their hands from the bucket. This done, in trying to leave the area, Mr Bick put his foot through the ceiling and his daughter fell into the bedroom below, landing on her back, half across a bed, sustaining minor injuries and a good shaking up. The attack by incendiaries had ended but high explosive bombs were now falling, giving rise to a number of incidents in the post's immediate vicinity and knocking out all telephone links between the control room, the wardens' posts and rescue depots. A high explosive bomb fell immediately opposite Post B 13 destroying three houses and Charity was told to take a message to the control room in West Bromwich Town Hall, more than half a mile away, asking for help. Borrowing a bicycle she set off but, on the way, had to dismount and lie in the gutter five times to avoid the effects of bombs falling nearby.

The sole medium of communication, she made the journey three times during the most intensive part of the raid covering one and a quarter miles, then a further journey of half a mile in a different direction towards Mayers Green, from her post to the reserve control room in Pitt Street and, from there, plastered in dirt and mud, to the control room – another half-mile journey. At that time four very large fires were blazing in the town and she had to pass in close proximity to all of them under a continual rain of high explosive bombs and shell fragments. After the raid finished she stayed at the post for the remainder of the night in physical pain, limping very badly at the end. Except when she was actually cycling on her duties she carried out, calmly and efficiently, tasks which released for other duties, wardens who would otherwise have been unavailable. On 17 June 1941 she went to Buckingham Palace where she was invested with her George Medal by HM The King – the youngest female up to date to receive it.

Charity Bick, who was fourteen at the time, had adopted a subterfuge normally limited to under-age candidates for the armed forces – she had falsely declared herself to be older and when the incident took place, was in fact one month short of her fifteenth birthday. She was born in Selly

Oak Hospital, Birmingham on 19 December 1925. Her father was the head gardener at Birmingham University and she was to have a younger brother. She went to school, in turn, at St. Benedict's Infant School, Small Heath, Lynge Lane Girls' School and Cronehill Central School before being evacuated to Lichfield, Staffordshire. Returning from there to Cronehill she left to work for a firm of manufacturing chemists at Oldbury and a large retail store in Birmingham where she was employed at the date that she became an ARP messenger (May/June 1940) and continued there until she joined the Women's Auxiliary Air Force (WAAF) at the second attempt in September 1943.

Her arrival at Wilmslow, Cheshire caused some discussion when she was seen to be wearing, as a recruit, a gallantry medal ribbon. She was trained as an electrician at RAF Melksham, Wiltshire but, finding that this limited her chances of advancement, she was reclassified in the Administration Branch on a course at Hawkinge, Kent. Having been posted and promoted at regular intervals throughout her service she finished at Northwood, Middlesex as a warrant officer after twenty-two years' service. On leaving the WRAF (as it had then become) she took up employment at the Atomic Energy Research Centre and then transferred, in 1967, to the Department of Health and Social Security at Didcot before being posted to Forres, Morayshire (now Grampian Region) where she now lives, having retired in 1987.

The same attack on the borough, after a quiet, cold day, also affected West Bromwich and District General Hospital in Edward Street where, by 7.30 p.m., large fires had started in two nearby buildings, one of which was the hospital laundry. They then set alight the roofs of two swimming baths on the opposite side of the street, creating a situation in which the hospital had extensive fires on two sides with a railway cutting occupying the third, leaving only one route for evacuation.

On 9 March 1887 Mary Thomas (née Parnell, formerly Johnson) had given birth to a daughter, Evalyn Gertrude, at Cowley St. John, Oxford. This baby was the younger daughter of the headmaster of

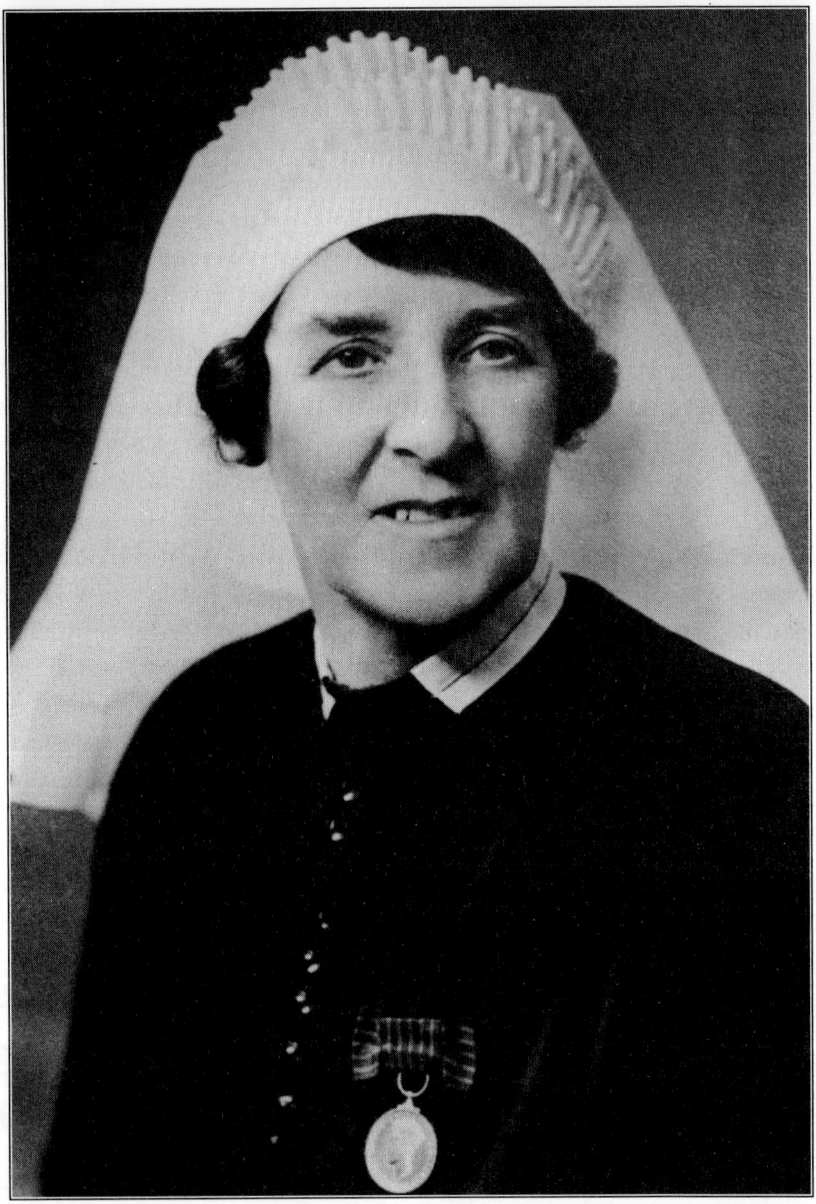

Miss Evalyn G. Thomas GM
(photo: R. & S. Shepherd).

St. John's School, Robert Thomas, MA (later Professor of Theology) – there was also a brother. After being tutored privately at home she attended St. Faith's private school then the convent school in Wellington Square, Oxford and between 1909 and 1912 trained at Bristol Royal Infirmary, qualifying SRN. She then nursed at Northampton General Hospital, Birmingham General Hospital and Queen's Hospital in the same city before joining the staff at West Bromwich to be appointed matron on 1 May 1924.

At the same time that she was arranging for patients at the danger points to be removed **Miss Evalyn Gertrude Thomas**, now forty-three years old, was dealing with a fire among furniture as well as incendiary bombs in the central residents' quarters. Single-handedly, she saved the centre block of the hospital where, had a fire developed, one of the main lines of retreat would have been cut off.

Dr W.S. Walton, the Medical Officer of Health for West Bromwich, having been engaged elsewhere and seen the glare of flames, arrived on the scene and, after a tour of the hospital, was discussing the position with Miss Thomas when three high explosive bombs struck in Lambard Street. One fell on the hospital laundry, completing demolishing it and blowing doctor and matron several yards in opposite directions. Picking herself up, she retrieved her cap and replaced it carefully and calmly on her head. Then, the doctor having ordered evacuation of the hospital, she set about organising and supervising this activity. With the help of private transport and two buses from which the seats had been ripped out this proceeded perfectly smoothly, without confusion, everybody following her example of courage and quietly efficient leadership.

Over several hours in the midst of the flames, smoke and benumbing noise, ninety-one patients were transferred safely to the Hallam Hospital (now replaced by the Sandwell General Hospital). It was due to her efforts that, amid scenes of potential and actual disaster, no lives were lost; only three nurses were wounded and three patients suffered minor injuries. When she returned to work next morning she insisted that the union flag be raised above the shattered hospital – a manifestation of her intense loyalty to country and profession. She was invested with her medal by HM The King at Buckingham Palace on 17 June 1941, Dr Walton receiving his George Medal at the same ceremony. She was to fill her responsible position for twenty-one years before retiring on 21 July 1945.

About medium height, slim with a serene demeanour, without doubt she had received a calling to her caring profession and was a woman of outstanding quality possessed of a deep understanding of human nature allied to a keen sense of humour. A truly saintly personality, her interests were tennis and needlework and a deep involvement in all church activities.

After retirement she went to live with her brother and sister in Gerards Cross, Buckinghamshire, then, some time later, both sisters moved to a house in south-east Oxford where Winifred died in 1959 after a serious illness. In the difficult task of nursing her sister Miss Thomas was helped by Miss Pauline L.M. Clark, a nurse who had previously been one of the staff at West Bromwich. When Miss Thomas became the victim of a serious heart defect Miss Clark went to live with her and both ladies moved to a flat in north Oxford in 1962. Her brother Robert having also predeceased her, Miss Thomas died in the Radcliffe Infirmary on 7 December 1972 and was buried four days later at St. Mary and St. John Church, Cowley Road in the parish of Cowley St. John. Miss Clark still survives, mentally alert, in Dudley, aged ninety-five.

When her medal appeared on the market in 1976 it was purchased by the chairman of the Sandwell Health Authority – a local business man – and is now displayed at Sandwell Nurses' District Training School in the old Hallam Hospital, West Bromwich in a special area together with a number of presentation addresses and a description of her courageous actions.

For Coventry the welcome, even essential, lull which had lasted from the previous November ended with severe air attacks on the three successive nights of 8, 9 and 10 April 1941 during which the Coventry and Warwickshire Hospital, at the junction of Stoney Stanton Road and Foleshill Road, was badly damaged. In the raid which started about 9 p.m. on Tuesday 8th, 237 aircraft dropped 315 tons of high explosive bombs and parachute mines and nearly 1,600 incendiary canisters, many falling on the hospital. When the first incendiaries fell on the Out-Patient Department and the Enquiry Office **Miss Joyce Elizabeth Burton**, the forty-four-year-old matron, made a full round of the nurses' homes telling her staff to report to their posts after which, as the high explosive bombs were by then falling, she continued her tour of inspection in the resuscitation ward and emergency theatres, checking the patients, encouraging staff and ensuring that everybody was ready to receive casualties. Continuing her rounds she could see that fires were breaking out and the bombers were using the hospital as an aiming mark so she carried on organising the work. After a bomb destroyed the X-Ray Department, killing two nurses on duty there, the electricity supply failed.

Bombs continued to explode, causing damage and inflicting casualties among staff and patients. There was also machine-gunning, and Miss Burton had to throw herself flat before continuing her duties calmly and efficiently, leading by example always. Two large surgical wards were now hit and patients were pinned down by shattered masonry, broken beds and bedding making it difficult to extricate them in the semi-darkness but the work of evacuating them to the basement continued despite further casualties. Having crossed a temporary plank bridge over one bomb crater the bomb detonated with a roar and, after an initial movement away, she returned and went down the crater to help members of her staff buried there. With rescuers now arriving she took a major part in tending the injured, for a time acting as stretcher bearer.

Although the raid ended at 4.30 a.m. rescue work went on throughout the day until 4 p.m. during which time she had the harrowing experience of identifying bodies of her own staff for, in addition to two doctors, two staff nurses and three probationers had been killed and fourteen injured. When this work had been completed she arranged transport for all her staff to accommodation at Keresley and

Kenilworth where they could have a well-earned rest. Recommended at first for the OBE this decision was changed at the Regional Commissioner level to the BEM but better judgement prevailed and she attended an investiture on 4 November 1941 to be presented, at Buckingham Palace, with the George Medal by HM The King.

In the late nineteenth century Mr Harry Alma Burton, a draper, and his wife Elizabeth Sarah (née Squires) lived in Searle Street, Chesterton in the northern part of Cambridge, the university city, and it was here that Joyce Elizabeth was born to them on 27 November 1896. After normal schooling she trained at the Norfolk and Norwich Hospital from 1918 to 1921, qualifying SRN on 15 June 1923 having completed her midwifery training at the Royal Staffordshire Hospital. She was appointed matron of the Coventry and Warwickshire Hospital in 1938 and retired in 1951. Returning to Cambridge she lived in Pretoria Road and died there on 22 February 1962.

During the same air-raid **Miss Emma Horne** (known as 'Pat'), a forty-year-old nursing sister, was on duty on the hospital's second floor when a direct hit by a high explosive bomb carried away the end of her ward – the Henry Johnson Ward. Exercising a calming influence by sheer personality she spared no effort in evacuating the patients to the greater safety of the basement. Two other wards then took direct hits so she went to them immediately and, disregarding personal danger, started to pull the patients from the wreckage and remove them to a safe area. Later, a concealed delayed action bomb detonated and she came across a junior nurse trapped under debris whom she managed to release. Then, in a situation of grave danger, she remained with her until further help arrived in the shape of morphia and a stretcher which the sister helped to carry to another ward. This bomb had caused great havoc with many casualties among the patients who had already been evacuated to the basement so Sister Horne worked unceasingly in dreadful conditions helping with casualties who were taken from there to the Pathology Department where they were kept for many hours waiting to be moved to a safer place.

She laboured for several hours in helping with the evacuation until late in the afternoon when transport arrived to take the nursing staff to homes in Kenilworth and Keresley. The hospital proposed the award of the MBE but her recommendation by the Regional Commissioner's staff was again for the BEM. Nevertheless, she was invested with her George Medal by HM The King at Buckingham Palace on 4 November 1941, the House Governor and Secretary of the hospital, Mr S.C. Hill, receiving a similar award for his gallantry during the raid.

'Pat' Horne was born on 17 March 1901 at Eglwsilan, Pontypridd in Glamorgan, the daughter of William Horne, a haulage contractor, who also had two sons and two other daughters. Educated at Pontypridd Grammer School, after service in the SJAB she trained from 1931 to 1935 at the Coventry and Warwickshire Hospital, qualifying later in midwifery. In 1937 she was promoted to Ward Sister, serving in that capacity until her retirement in 1961 after which she returned, part time, as Administrative Sister. She died in the same hospital on 5 May 1968 and, following a service in the United Church, was cremated at Cranley Garden Cemetery, her ashes being scattered at Glynstaff Cemetery, Pontypridd.

Taller than the average, she was a dedicated, kind and caring nurse throughout her career, possessed of a good sense of humour and devoted to the training and well-being of student nurses. Privately she was interested in needlework, travelling and cooking. After her death, at the request of the family, her medal was placed on display in the International Chapel of Walsgrave Hospital, Coventry in a memorial cabinet but it disappeared during renovation.

Gallantry awards were not on this occasion confined to the professional staff for **Mrs Mary Dirinda Julia Beardshall** (published in *London Gazette Supplement* as 'May'), a twenty-eight-year-old mother of three girls and a boy, working as a hospital portress, was on duty throughout the night. When the air-raid started she was operating the telephone switchboard and a high explosive bomb exploded outside from which she received head injuries. A short time later she was on the top floor of the building putting out, on her own, a fire caused by incendiaries, using only her hands and some sand. She prevented the spread of flames to furniture and mattresses which had been thrown about by the explosions then, clambering through the debris, she helped an injured man to safety. Although she had been injured herself by falling rubble she followed this by supporting a beam while several patients were extricated.

Climbing along a ledge to Alexandra Ward she helped rescue other patients trapped beneath blocks of concrete, facilitating their removal to the basement by stretcher before a delayed action bomb detonated causing injuries to her scalp and face. There further injuries caused her to collapse so she was transferred to hospital in Bromsgrove, south-west of Birmingham, where she was admitted suffering also from severe shock. She remained unconscious for six of the ten weeks that she was a patient and, after discharge, was appointed doctor's registration clerk in the out-patients' department, the only part of the hospital remaining. She received her medal from HM The King at Buckingham Palace on 21 July 1941.

Born at Barby, near Rugby, Warwickshire on 28 October 1912, one of three children of Frederick Foster, a farm worker, and Julia (née Buckley) she spent practically all of her childhood with her paternal grandparents at Hill Morton, a small village on the eastern outskirts of Rugby where she went to school. When her school days were over she worked as a tailor's presser and on 31 December 1930, at Rugby Registry Office, married Lewis Beardshall, a pattern maker employed at Armstrong-Whitworth, the heavy engineering and car firm. Later, she was employed in the blueprint department of British Thomson-Houston, electrical engineers, in Rugby before spending several years working in Wellhouse Hospital, Barnet and St. Bartholomew's Hospital, London prior to starting as a portress.

After a spell as a clerk she enlisted in the Auxiliary Territorial Service (ATS) at Bolton-upon-Dearne, Yorkshire and, by the end of the war, had risen to the rank of Regimental Sergeant Major (RSM) in a mixed anti-aircraft regiment on Hayling Island near Portsmouth.

After demobilisation she worked for the West End cosmetics firm, Elizabeth Arden, where her fine knowledge of four languages was to be of value. Nothing has been heard of her for more than forty years although the opinion has been advanced that she may have gone to the continent of Europe.

Margaret Brown was born on 26 March 1919 at University College Hospital, Bloomsbury, London, one of two children of William George Brown and his wife Mary (still alive at the age of ninety-four). Mr Brown served for eighteen years in the Royal Garrison Artillery and won the Military Medal at Ypres. He was discharged in 1920 to work first as a miner before moving to the Coventry area, where the family settled in the village of Longford. He went to work for Sterling Metals Ltd. and retired as traffic manager after thirty-seven years. Margaret attended Foxford Council School in Longford, leaving in 1933 at the age of fourteen to start work at Alfred Herbert Ltd., a machine tool manufacturer. Her family moved from the Croft, Lady Lane, Longford to Hen Lane in 1936 in which year she joined the SJAB Holbrooks Division. When she started work at Herbert's she joined the works SJAB unit with which she worked by day and was part of the division by night.

On the night of the 10th a dwelling house in Hen Lane, Coventry was struck by a high explosive bomb and the back wall was blown in, three people being trapped when the roof collapsed. Margaret, the twenty-two-year-old works nurse, on her way to check her parents' safety, passed the scene and heard a sound so she crawled under the roof which was then in an unstable condition about two feet from the ground. In considerable danger she tunnelled in through the debris and reached a nineteen-year-old youth with whom, although she could have backed out and saved herself, she stayed for over an hour. She spent this time talking to him and giving him comfort until the rescue party, driving in from the other side, arrived and was able to extricate them both although bombs were falling throughout and the rubble had collapsed. Sadly, the youth died as soon as he was brought clear.

Later on in the same night the Holbrooks St. John's Ambulance

Brigade Hall in Wheelwright Lane received a direct hit by a high explosive bomb which caused many casualties and, working for many hours despite the heavy bombing, she attended these with such skill that many lives were saved. During previous raids she had rendered consistently brave and efficient service inspiring all to greater efforts. She was recommended for the BEM but this was amended and, on 4 November 1941, she was invested with the George Medal by HM The King at Buckingham Palace.

In 1942, at Keresley Church, she married John Stowe, a machine driller at the Daimler Motor Works, and set up home in Keresley village about a mile to the west of her parents' home and lived there until John's death in 1971. She then moved to Wardsworth Road, Bedworth, a small town across the M6 motorway, and still lives there, virtually housebound. She is still living through a legacy of that night in 1941 for, in addition to the George Medal, when the rubble collapsed she collected spinal neck injuries. As a demonstration of her regard for the help that the people of Bedworth had given her she presented her medal to the town where it is displayed in a showcase in the civic hall, the presentation to the mayor having been made in October 1985 at a civic reception. Forced by her injury to give up her beloved SJAB activities when she was thirty-one, her association with that organisation continues through one of her sons who is superintendent at Area Headquarters in Coventry.

Born in Reddish, Stockport (now Greater Manchester) on 21 April 1915, **Vera Anderson** was taken to Nottingham in 1918 when her father, Arthur Gorst Anderson, started work at Boots', eventually becoming a foreman in the saccharin factory at Beeston, south of the city. Educated at Nottingham Clarendon School for Girls she started work in the audit department of Boot's Pure Drug Co. Ltd. but could not settle to office work so, hearing of a vacancy in their central surgery, she applied for and underwent two years' training in which she showed promise of becoming an excellent nurse. She suffered a major disappointment in 1934 when her application to take general nursing training at Nottingham Central Hospital was turned down on the grounds that, at 4′ 10½″, she was below the minimum height but, after an appeal emphasising her special qualities, she was accepted.

During her training she won the prize for the best all-round nurse of the year then, in 1938, after passing her final state examination, she qualified for a one-year scholarship for training under the Central Midwives Board. Having spent six months each at Leeds and Manchester on this course she took up employment on the nursing staff of the Central Surgery in August 1940.

After midnight on 8/9 May 1941 (Thursday night) nearly a hundred enemy bombers, tasked to attack Derby, actually delivered their bomb loads on Nottingham fifteen miles to the east and then, after debriefing and re-arming, the next wave dropped its lethal cargo onto open fields the same distance further east.

After the first attack fires were raging and roads were blocked in the area of Boot's Surgery in Station Street, south of Nottingham Canal, and Miss Anderson, who was on duty at the time of the air-raid alert, had been on duty since 8 a.m. the previous day and was on her way up to the ground floor with first aid equipment. The building was set on fire by one or more hits so, returning to the basement, she tried to telephone the ARP Central Control but found that the line had been put out of action. She therefore started to deal with her first casualty, Mr William Daykin, a night watchman and firewatcher, who had been severely injured. He had collapsed so she gave him first aid, calling for blankets, hot water bottles and a kettle of hot water which would have to be obtained from the third floor as other sources had been cut off by further explosions.

Accompanied by another firewatcher, Mr William Ellis, she made for the third floor surgery using the staircase which was in total darkness but, during the return journey, another bomb explosion threw her violently against the wall. Undeterred, she resumed Mr Daykin's treatment but by this time, water was pouring into the basement from a burst water main, the upper floors had collapsed and burning material was dropping from the ceiling. A door which had been blown off its hinges was recovered to serve as a makeshift stretcher for the badly injured man and, with the help of firewatchers, she succeeded in fighting her way through the chaos to have him carried to the back of the building and thence to a railway arch, extinguishing several incendiaries herself on the way. After she had tried, unsuccessfully, to summon an ambulance for Mr Daykin with whom she stayed until he died, she returned to the yard to see if she could be of further help but, with three other firewatchers buried completely under fallen masonry, she decided to reach the central control room in Island Street.

This had also suffered damage but, the direct route being impassable because of fierce flames, she succeeded in reaching it by a circuitous route, fully half a mile longer, in the continuing air-raid, arriving wet through and covered in dust and dirt. Seriously affected by the strain of her exertions but still carrying her first aid kit, this diminutive woman paused only long enough to wash and have a cup of tea before dealing with twenty casualties, six of whom she caused to be evacuated to the clearing station in Queen's Drive. She treated the minor cuts and abrasions of the remainder herself, arranged for them to be given hot drinks, and then supervised the clearing up of the First Aid Post.

However, spreading flames from the adjacent building forced her to move yet again with her equipment to one of the shelters where she dealt with minor casualties as they arrived. Miss Anderson worked under heavy pressure from 1.30 a.m. until she was relieved at 7.30 a.m. then continued to discharge various duties until mid-day at which time she was sent home to Ebors Road, to return only two days later. The virtues of great efficiency, resource, cheerfulness, coolness and heroism had all been fully demonstrated in the terrifying period through which this pretty blue-eyed twenty-six-year-old and every other survivor had passed. She received her medal from HM The King at Buckingham Palace on 7 December 1941.

On 15 August 1942 she married Dr Lockhart, a staff doctor who had also been in charge of the Emergency Medical Service for the City of Nottingham. He later took up general practice in Chester, moving still later to Cornwall where she bore him two children, both of whom survive. She died on 13 October 1963 and, after cremation, her ashes were taken back to the Garden of Rest in Wilford Hill Crematorium in Nottingham where her name is engraved in the Book of Remembrance.

Aberdeen, the city at the mouth of the Rivers Dee and Don, was the county town of Aberdeenshire and a significant fishing port, one of Scotland's Royal Burghs engaged in shipbuilding, engineering and chemical production and other industries. Known, for obvious reasons, as 'The Granite City' it is on the east coast and is the centre of the North Sea oil industry. In 1942 it had a population of 165,000 and on the night of 7 August it was subjected to yet another hit-and-run air-raid, one or two aircraft dropping high explosive bombs. One of them fell on a four-storey granite tenement building at 214 Market Street at its junction with Poynderwood Road, resulting in a fire breaking out in the ground floor. **Mrs Marion Patterson**, a senior volunteer fire guard for the preceding three months based at Civil Defence HQ at Marischal Street, appeared on the scene immediately to find that the fire amid the debris was intensifying. So, her slim figure enabling her to penetrate farther than the men on the spot, she crawled into the debris with the stirrup pump and extinguished the flames before they could take hold and escalate to the level of a major conflagration.

Shortly afterwards, before the arrival of the rescue party, she heard that a naval rating, Alexander James Chisholm, was trapped in the debris. He was one of a sizeable naval party guarding an ammunition dump in the vicinity. He was in a particularly difficult position so, volunteering to help, she burrowed fifteen feet into the heavy granite wreckage then downwards for several feet until she reached the man whom she found confined in a more or less upright position with his head about six feet below the surface. With Mrs Patterson directing the rescue work from her position near him it was found that he could not be pulled up because his legs were trapped by a beam across his thighs. She then burrowed farther down after which he was drawn up by another rescuer who, suspended downwards by those on top, was able to grasp the sailor's shoulders. He made a good recovery and went back to sea but, tragically, his ship was torpedoed and lost with all hands. The minute after she had crawled clear of the debris to refresh herself at a water hydrant it collapsed, completely filling the cavities in which she had been working. She was invested with her medal by HM The King at Buckingham Palace on 23 February 1943.

Marion Patterson (née Chalmers) was born in 1911 in Aberdeen and her early years were spent in Fairbank, a small town in Ontario, Canada where she attended Fairbank Public School. Afterwards she was employed at Simpson's Knitting Mill in Toronto. During the Second World War she crossed the Atlantic where she was involved in the Market Street incident. She returned to Canada after the war and was the subject of a popular welcome party in Yorktownship, Ontario of which Fairbank formed part. She made a further visit to Aberdeen in September 1985 which was covered by an article in the *Aberdeen Evening Express*. She still lives in Ontario.

Chapter 4

Air-Raids – Overseas

As THE war spread to areas of the world outside Europe, the Middle East and Russia, air attacks were mounted by the Axis Powers in regions not previously under threat, even some that had, hitherto, not even seen any type of aircraft. After the Japanese capture of Hong Kong on Christmas Day 1941 news of the atrocities committed there by the invaders, sated with conquest, against nurses and others leaked out and the city of Singapore was among those places where this intelligence became known. Following the avalanche of Japanese victories in their advance down the four hundred miles of the Malayan peninsula the prospect of Singapore's capture and occupation had to be contemplated. Then, in early February, this expectation hardened into certainty with the accompanying conclusion that the barbarities of Hong Kong would be repeated when the battle-hardened Japanese arrived.

The essential evacuation of civilians and non-effectives was already in train when the Principal Matron, Miss V.M.S. James, QAIMNS (who was to die on 14 February aboard the Auxiliary Patrol Vessel *Kuala*) was trying to implement the secret order of Lieutenant General A.E. Percival, General Officer Commanding Malaya, that half the nurses – military and civilian – should leave. She called for volunteers but without success so she was faced with making the awesome, potentially life or death decision of selecting the fifty per cent herself. On 12 February 1942, three days before the island fortress fell, the Blue Funnel MV *Gorgon* with HMT *Empire Star* (Blue Star Line but originally owned by Frederick Leyland & Co. Ltd) in company sailed in daylight with a naval escort of the cruiser HMS *Durban* (4,850 tons) and the 2,499-ton Straits Steam Ship Co's HMS *Kedah*, an auxiliary destroyer. They were heading for Batavia on the island of Java in the Dutch East Indies (now Indonesia) with the *Empire Star* carrying over 2,200 people, accommodated mostly in holds designed to hold refrigerated meat. Among them were soldiers, sailors, airmen, deserters, civilians – men, women and children – crew and more than a hundred nurses. These included nursing staff from Nos. 2/10 and 2/13 Australian General Hospitals, one from the latter being **Staff Nurse Margaret Irene Anderson** ('Margaret' only in *London Gazette Supplement*), Australian Army Nursing Service.

When the 12,656-ton *Empire Star* reached the southern end of the Durian Strait between the east coast of Sumatra and the Rhio Archipelago she was attacked by Japanese dive bombers. These attacks, by a total of 57 aircraft, extending intermittently over four hours, succeeded in hitting the ship three times, twelve military personnel being killed and seventeen seriously injured. Fires were started and Miss Anderson, with some other nursing officers, was in a cabin with some severely wounded men who were being badly affected by smoke and fumes. Thinking that the attack had finished, she helped to drag the men out onto the deck only for another aircraft to strike, machine-gunning the ship. Showing complete disregard for her own safety, she remained on deck, sheltering the patients who had been badly injured, protecting one by throwing herself across him.

Because, at the appropriate time, she was serving in a hospital ship, her George Medal was not presented to her but was sent from the Governor General of Australia's office on 12 March 1945. One CBE, two OBEs, three MBEs, two BEMs and two Commendations were awarded to the ship's officers and crew for their work in the escape.

The *Empire Star* disembarked RAF personnel at Tanjong Priok, Batavia and reached Fremantle, Western Australia but did not survive the war, being sunk on 23 October 1942 at position 48°14′N, 26°22′W, 950 miles west of Ushant, where a submarine torpedoed her. The other nurses left Singapore on the following day on the Sarawak SS Co's 1,670-ton SS *Vyner Brooke* which did not fare so well as she was bombed and sunk fifteen miles north of Muntok, Banks Island, off the south-west coast of Sumatra. Among the pitifully small number of survivors that reached the island, more than twenty Australian nurses were brutally murdered on the beach by the Japanese, the rest being taken into captivity where many died before the end of the war could bring liberation.

Born in Melbourne, Victoria on 11 December 1915, Miss Anderson trained at the Austin Hospital, Heidelburg and the Royal Women's Hospital, Carlton, both in Melbourne, then, after qualifying, joined the AANS as a staff nurse on 3 October 1940. Her first posting was to 2/13 Australian General Hospital in Malaya, and she served throughout the short campaign until evacuation, being promoted to Sister Group 2 on 1 December 1941 then Sister Group 1 on 7 July 1942, by which time she had reached safety in Australia. On re-assignment she joined HMAHS *Wanganella* (2/2), which had earlier transported 2/13 AGH to Singapore in mid-September 1941. This vessel was to have an impressive war record, handling thousands of casualties; during Miss Anderson's service in her the 9,576-ton converted Huddart Parker Ltd's liner dealt with casualties from Milne Bay, New Guinea, the Solomon Islands and Borneo, with a special voyage to pick up New Zealanders from Taranto in the heel of Italy.

In mid-April 1944 the ship was involved in dealing with casualties arising from the massive explosion of the Port Line's 7,142-ton munition ship SS *Fort Stikine* in Bombay harbour, India, her staff performing vital surgery before handing the patients on to civilian hospitals ashore. Margaret Anderson remained in the Sister Group 1 grade until 22 March 1943 when she was commissioned Lieutenant in the AANS on the following day and seconded to the Australian Imperial Forces (AIF) on the same date (see page 148). On 6 April 1945 she was posted from *Wanganella* to 115 (Heidelberg) Military Hospital, Melbourne arriving on 8 August. She was placed on the Retired Service List on 12 February 1946 and married after the war, becoming Mrs O'Bryan.

She now lives in Frankston, Victoria south of Melbourne on the western shore of Port Philip Bay.

Thursday 22 January 1942, almost four weeks before Singapore fell, saw the Japanese crossing the border from Siam (Thailand) into Burma to start their advance on India, their tactical methods recalling the German *Blitzkrieg* – savage aerial attack ahead of the thrust of ground forces. In spite of a fighting retreat by the Burma Army the Japanese made rapid progress northwards and, just after 10 a.m. on 12 April, two waves of Japanese bombers hit Taunggyi, a hill station in Central Burma, ninety miles south-south-east of Mandalay. For hour after hour the bamboo and timber town was attacked with high explosive and anti-personnel bombs, two hospitals particularly, the Military Hospital in the Old Shan Chiefs' School and the single storey brick and stone Civil Hospital, being targeted. When the latter was hit, **Miss Helen Rodriguez** (mis-spelt 'Hellen' in *London Gazette Supplement*), the matron, was giving post-operative treatment to an elderly man. Machine gun bullets shattered the windows without warning, slivers of glass flying in all directions, so she pulled him onto a mattress on the floor then protected him with her body.

Born on 24 October 1914 at a remote hill station in the Chin Hills, north Burma, Helen Rodriguez was the elder of two daughters of Lambert Kenneth Rodriguez, a Portuguese who came from Travancore, India. Gaining a medical degree and gold medal at Madras University he then studied in Edinburgh and qualified FRCS(Ed) in 1905, having been admitted LRCP, LRCS(Ed), LRCS(Glasgow) and DPH in the previous year. While in Edinburgh he fell in love with Mary Stewart-More Hunter, a daughter of Dr James Hunter, teacher and examiner in physiology at the university and Royal College of Surgeons, Edinburgh as well as at Minto House School of Medicine. They were married at St. Columba's Roman Catholic Church, Newington in the city on 27 June 1912 where he is described in the register as District Medical Officer, Burma. When Helen was old enough she attended Kingswood School, Kalewa (broken by a year in Edinburgh) then trained at Rangoon General Hospital where she qualified SRN, being appointed to Taunggyi as matron at the remarkably early age of twenty-six.

The next few hours were occupied with the treatment of a variety of wounds resulting from the attack but her otherwise unremitting preoccupation with medical care was broken during the day when her attention was drawn to an unexploded aircraft bomb. An American scientific magazine, recently arrived, had included an article on these munitions and their disposal so, the garrison engineer being absent on duty, she succeeded in defusing the bomb guided by the information so fortuitously to hand. The raid was followed by shelling of the civilian market, resulting in more than four hundred new patients for her hospital, but that night the native doctors left and, fearful for their safety should the Japanese arrive, she persuaded the Shan nurses and her parents to leave also.

After that, despite further air-raids, she continued to tend many patients helped by just one woman until, faced by an ever-decreasing supply of medicine and drugs, they were both working like sleep-walkers. The military hospital was the prime target in a subsequent bombardment days later and, when a messenger arrived asking for help, she ran there although shells were falling in the vicinity. In the absence of stretcher bearers she carried badly wounded Indian soldiers to safety on her back although herself weak from lack of food. One of these soldiers was a twelve-stone Pathan well over six feet tall but, despite shell fire, she took him to a slit trench. Then, having transferred the Pathan from there to her own hospital, she was repeating the action with another soldier when she sustained a bullet or shell fragment wound in her leg.

Picking up this man again she succeeded in her mission and, helped by the woman and, unexpectedly, a male tubercular patient, she completed the prodigious task of transferring all the wounded soldiers without any form of transport, taking four days to do so. During a further period of bombardment, while European soldiers buried the many corpses, she performed many operations, including a leg amputation, with practically no sleep. When these soldiers were finally ordered away she refused to make good her escape, preferring to accompany her charges into captivity. During the period of waiting she had to shoot two Japanese soldiers, looters intent on rape, and dispose of their bodies, then, before she was taken prisoner, endure days of extreme danger while Japanese troops fought over the ground.

In the following weeks she managed to rescue her father, who had refused to leave Burma, then started a journey to Maymyo which was long and tortuous, although, in direct line, it was only seventy miles away, and set up a service as unofficial district nurse to the local population. She went, later, to Rangoon for some time and then to Barabattia, a small Gurkha village six miles from Maymyo, where she continued her caring activities until 7 September 1943 when she was taken forcibly to Mandalay by the Kempetei, the Japanese secret police – an oriental Gestapo. Here she was to earn her George Medal over again because her mother, in all innocence, had notified her, via the Red Cross, of her award; this information was taken by her captors to be a military decoration for spying activities. For thirty-one days she was kept in a tiny, foul-smelling cell under solitary confinement except for those periods when she was being interrogated, beaten or tortured. Released, she returned to the Gurkha village but later, she was sent to an internment camp at Maymyo filled with men, women and children in a pitiful state and commanded by a sadistic officer.

Freed by the advancing British army on 11 March 1945, she directed her energies to helping bombed and burned villagers before falling victim to cholera which laid her low for several weeks. After considerable frustration with the slowness of the official procedure she managed to organise her father's return to India but he died in Calcutta soon after arrival there. Driven by the unquenchable flame of service she went to work among lepers in nearby Mandalay, not reaching Bangalore, India until 1 July 1945 where she was reunited with her mother. With considerable reluctance occasioned by the bureaucratic treatment that her father had suffered after their release at Maymyo she agreed to go to Secunderabad, Hyderabad State where, on 11 October 1946, she was presented with her George Medal by The Honourable Resident, Sir Arthur Cunningham Lothian, KCSI, CIE, at the Residency.

After Indian Independence had been declared in 1947 she worked in Ootacamund, Madras Presidency in 1950, Secunderabad and elsewhere in southern India, then, later, worked for a medical missionary, Dr Ida Scudder, at Vellore Christian Medical School where she was involved in running a medical van service to isolated villages. After this she also worked with Sister Theresa in the slums of Calcutta, giving aid and comfort to the homeless and destitute before visiting Kyoto, Japan to keep a promise made during her captivity. In 1974 she fell and broke her leg in Bangalore, Mysore, India to become permanently wheelchair bound although this did not diminish her zest for life. In 1953 she had married a Yorkshire/Parsee motor dealer, Mr Prestonji, in Burma but he died leaving her a widow before she came to the United Kingdom in 1975 to stay with her sister Isabel who was working at Heathrow Airport and living at Whitton, near Hounslow.

While visiting her niece in Epsom in 1977 she suffered a heart attack and had to be admitted to Epsom District Hospital after which, her accommodation no longer being available, she had to be rehoused. She was to spend six months with her niece before going to live in a flat on the edge of Hounslow Heath where she endured very poor health until her death on 16 June 1982. She remained cheerful in the face of adversity, so proud of her Scottish ancestry that she wore her father's tartan at all times and observed her religious beliefs in the Church of Scotland. Her abiding interests were children, animals, cooking and fishing to which she gave her whole-hearted support. She was cremated in the South West Middlesex Crematorium on 23 June, her ashes being flown to India and, as she had requested, scattered on the hills at Kodaikanal, where she had worked, in the Palmi Hills, near Solheim, South Madras Presidency. From the time of her marriage she had adopted the name Mrs Helen Preston.

With the American 5th Army in Italy held up at Cassino and in the Liri Valley by the Gustav Line, part of the *Winterstellung* (Winter Position), the Allied drive on Rome was running out of steam early in 1944 so Operation *Shingle* was set in motion. A left hook to get around behind the German defences and open the way to the 'Holy City', this ambitious undertaking consisted of an American/British landing on 22 January over the beaches north and south of Anzio. This was a small resort and fishing port on the west coast in the province of Lazio, access being gained through the Tyrrhenian Sea. The initial assault was completely successful in taking the Germans off balance, but excessive caution by the American force commander caused the operation to lose its momentum. The Germans reacted quickly and, with four divisions counter-attacking, the Allied initiative was lost and the invasion forces were in great danger of being pushed ignominiously back into the sea.

The operation having been mounted in the depth of the Italian winter, the terrain had already assumed the nightmare quality of France and Flanders in the First World War although a very short period of aerial and land bombardment had passed. With the campaign developing as far as shipping and landing craft availability would allow, reinforcements were crowding into an increasingly cramped area. The medical component of the British forces included No. 15 Casualty Clearing Station (CCS) RAMC and, because of heavy shelling and mortaring, their tents were dug in with little more than their roofs above ground. Owing to the abnormal proximity of the front line further protection was afforded by heaping the earth spoil as parados above them and the inclement weather meant that the ground was waterlogged and the tents were surrounded by mud flats.

This unit was squeezed into a small area further congested by the presence of two other CCSs, the American evacuation hospital and several field ambulances. In addition, No. 1 Reception Camp, Italy (the first destination of newly arrived troops) was at one end while safety was considerably prejudiced by the presence of an ammunition dump at the other end. With operational targets in close proximity it mattered not that the medical units were displaying the International Red Cross markings and at 6.45 a.m. on 14 March, enemy aircraft in considerable numbers machine-gunned and bombed No. 15 CCS and the reception camp. **Sister Sheila Margaret Greaves**, QAIMNS(R) was on duty in charge of the pre-operative ward which was at the end of a long

Lieut. (Sister) S. M. Greaves QAIMNS (R) GM
(photo: Imperial War Museum).

ward tent in a small, four-stretcher, resuscitation annexe in which oil stoves had to be used because of the cold.

Seeing that the bombs were falling clear of the CCS but were hitting the reception camp two hundred yards away, she ran to the bombed area in spite of the earth spouting up from bomb hits, being joined by three male officers. With them she started to dress the wounded, continuing to do so while a second wave of aircraft flew in, dropping anti-personnel bombs as well as heavily machine-gunning the area. She continued to work with the canvas overhead being torn apart by bullets, disregarding her own safety, and brought first aid relief to the casualties without waiting for them to be transferred to the CCS and was an inspiration to all in their ultimate evacuation.

Miss Greaves, whose father was the Bishop of Grimsby at the time of the award, was his second daughter, born on New Year's Day 1911. Educated at Kettering High School, Northamptonshire, she trained at Guy's Hospital in London, enlisting in Queen Alexandra's Imperial Military Nursing Service Reserve in 1938. After the outbreak of the Second World War she was in the first contingent to go to France with the British Expeditionary Force where she served with No. 2 General Hospital, RAMC and CCS West Force. Having been cut off with the 51st Highland Division at St. Valery-en-Caux, Département Seine Inférieure when the German forces overran France, she managed to leave Cherbourg in the last ship, one month after Dunkirk had been evacuated. A month later she left England again for Cape Town then served with No. 8 General Hospital in Syria, No. 2 CCS in the North African desert and No. 15 CCS in Sicily and Italy.

She returned home on 7 January 1945 after more than five years overseas, mostly in operational theatres of war apart from a short break following France. Because of her mother's death in December 1945 the original investiture arrangements had to be held over and she received her medal from HM The King at Buckingham Palace on 25 February 1946. After service in Lincoln and York military hospitals she was demobilised from the 'QAs' and was married at Lincoln in June 1948 to Humphrey Fox, a gunner major. They now live near Tunbridge Wells in Kent.

Chapter 5

Resistance/Underground – North-West Europe

SHORTLY after France's capitulation Winston Churchill, the Prime Minister, speaking to Dr Hugh Dalton, the Minister of Economic Warfare, about the formation of the Special Operations Executive (SOE) demanded, 'and now set Europe ablaze.' In north-west Europe Allied and neutral countries had become, progressively, enemy-occupied territories: Denmark on 9 April, Norway on 2 May, the Netherlands on 14 May, Belgium on 27 May and France on 25 June 1940; and thus were all potential targets for SOE activities, carried out by a mixture of all interested parties.

As far as British honours and decorations to clandestine forces were concerned, active operations in contact with the enemy attracted operational awards such as the DSO, MC, MM, etc., with the proviso that they should be 'honorary' where appropriate. For actions not directly in the face of the enemy a separate category of awards was available ranging from the George Cross, through the George Medal, the various grades of the Order of the British Empire to the King's Medal for Courage in the Cause of Freedom but the last two were not introduced until August 1945. Like the Victoria Cross, the George Cross could not be awarded to foreign nationals (but see p. 4 above) so some of the awards of the George *Medal* to them were for services normally considered worthy of the higher award.

Activities considered to come under the heading 'resistance/

underground' encompassed sabotage, intelligence gathering and transmission, facilitating escape and evasion, guerrilla warfare and maintenance of clandestine communications, all in occupied countries although not all necessarily in direct contact with the enemy. People engaged in these activities were, however, all under constant threat from him and his collaborators.

With Norway one of the first countries to be occupied by the Germans in 1940, SOE moved in quickly although, the country being at the extreme limit of parachute operations range, service direct from the United Kingdom had to be by sea. The town of Mosjøen is situated in Norland beside Vefsn Fiord on the east coast just south of the Arctic Circle and it was in this area that **Miss Liv Grannes** was the organisation's contact from 1940 to the autumn of 1942 at which stage she had to leave to escape the attentions of the Gestapo.

She was born in June 1918 in Mosjøen where her father was the headmaster of the local primary school which she attended when the time arrived. She went on to college at Orkdal Landsgymnasium near Trondheim, more than two hundred miles down the coast, following this with a period at the Oslo Social Workers' Academy. She was still a student when Norway was over-run and started her dangerous activities as an extra secretary in the police office on a temporary basis.

When the British forces left Norway in May 1940 after a disastrously ill-prepared campaign she found that, from her office in Mosjøen Police Station, she could carry on active warfare against the enemy by disinformation, falsifying police records, losing their letters and opening every one which looked as if it might be of interest. In July 1940 she succeeded in passing the intelligence so gained to the British Military Attaché in Stockholm, Sweden. By return, she was asked to provide the bearer with new identity cards which the Germans had brought into use so she issued these under various pseudonyms. A large number of people were soon travelling all over the country under cover of identity cards stamped and registered in the approved manner at Mosjøen Police Station. In addition to this, all kinds of useful documents and personal permits to reside, travel or trade in prohibited zones were being sent in blank to the British Legation in Sweden and passwords were established by means of which anyone could call for help while preparing for or escaping from illegal work and so find safe shelter and food.

In autumn 1940, she asked that a wireless telegraphy transmitter and operator be sent to her as well as arms for a band of resisters that she had gathered in her village, but it was impossible to send this until the spring of 1942. When the Archer/Heron mission from the United Kingdom arrived by fishing boat she gave them all the guidance and intelligence that they desired, providing them with special passes and arranging for some of them to be hidden at her uncle's remote farm. The party's leader reported that if it had not been for her it would not have been possible to land such a large party and infiltrate so many arms and so much equipment into the inhospitable countryside of north Norway in the middle of winter.

She was forced to leave the area towards the end of 1942 when a German patrol, having discovered a couple of British-trained instructors, was engaged by them and suffered casualties. After their escape the Gestapo began to suspect Liv Grannes' role and tapped her telephone then interrogated her so that it became obvious that she had to leave the country. A planned flying-boat pick-up having to be abandoned she was conducted over the mountains to Sweden from where she was transferred in turn to the United Kingdom by air, landing at Leuchars, Fife. On arrival, she provided much useful information about the area in which she had worked and was later appointed to Department FO IV of the Norwegian High Command.

Three other women of the Grannes family took an active part in the SOE organisation in Norland, a markedly positive demonstration of their detestation of the German invaders. Captain Birger Sjøberg, a Swede in the Norwegian army, married her in 1943 but he was killed in the Vefsn mountains by enemy patrols in a stern fight in June 1944. He was serving in the Norwegian Independent Company, known as the Linge Company after Captain Martin Linge, an outstanding leader who was killed in action in Norway. Commissioned into the Norwegian Armed Forces in 1944, Liv Granne was integrated with her department into the Norwegian section of SOE HQ. Her two brothers were to be among the loyal Norwegians captured by the Germans.

Her honorary George Medal was approved under the name of Liv Sjøberg on 22 July 1946 and she received it at the hands of His Britannic Majesty's Ambassador to the Norwegian Government, Sir Laurence Collier, KCMG. After the war she spent two years in specialised studies and was employed at the London School of Economics reading psychiatric social studies. She was occupied in this discipline at Oslo University Psychiatric Unit between 1952 and 1960, having married Jens Christian Hauge in 1958. He is a barrister at the Norwegian Supreme Court and they now live in Oslo, she having followed the Norwegian custom of adopting the combined name of Grannes-Hauge.

With the Germans victorious in The Netherlands, Belgium and France in such a short time span – 14 May to 25 June – and these countries having common frontiers, it will be convenient to deal with their territories as a whole* which indeed, they had become after assimilation into the Third Reich, albeit unwillingly for the most part.

A feature of the unexpectedly rapid German advance was their total lack of preparedness for the number of prisoners of war with which they were having to deal. Ideally, from the German point of view, they should all have been transported to the Fatherland as a bonus, unpaid, to the available slave labour force but that would take time and organisation to solve the massive logistical problems, even by German humanitarian standards, so advantage was taken of staging camps in convenient locations on the way.

One such camp was set up at Doulons, Département Somme, twenty miles west-south-west of Arras, Département Pas de Calais, where **Mrs Berthe Émilie Josephe Fraser** ('Berthe' only in *London*

* Those activities which were to some extent confined to southern France are dealt with in Chapter 6.

Gazette Supplement) was resident. Born in Behagnies (Pas de Calais) on 3 September 1894, the daughter of M. Clovis Vicogne and his wife Émilie (née Brunelle) she married a British ex-soldier, John Herbert Fraser, from St. Pancras, London who had been fighting throughout the First World War in the 8th Seaforth Highlanders. Holder of the MSM he had, at the age of twenty, been the youngest sergeant major in the British Army. After the marriage, by which she acquired British nationality, they set up a perfume business in Rue Saint Aubert, Arras but, when the Germans arrived in 1940, Fraser was interned at Loos-lez-Lisle, then in Upper Silesia, Germany and his wife organised a group of helpers who sent parcels of food, blankets and clothing to British prisoners of war at the Doulons camp.

When the camp closed down in January 1941 for the prisoners to be transferred to Pomerania in eastern Germany and Poland she, with a friend, evolved and carried out a plan of escapes by which they arranged the dispersal of many escapers after which they re-assembled them when possible, paying all expenses out of their own pockets. They were then passed to another friend and conducted to Port Vendres, Département Pyrenées Orientales on the Gulf of Lyons, on their way to the United Kingdom via Gibraltar. As a result of these activities she, with two friends, was betrayed by a French Quisling and arrested by the Gestapo on 11 September 1941, then incarcerated in Loos Prison, Liège, Limburg Province, Belgium while her friends were deported to Germany. She was held for fifteen months until 23 December 1942 but, after her release, did not hesitate to resume her dangerous work for the Resistance movement in the Arras district, contacting several officers who had been sent from England.

She organised and directed an extremely efficient intelligence *réseau* and provided shelter for agents and escaping personnel as well as for arms and explosives caches. In the month of November 1943 alone she sheltered in her own house a dozen Resistance leaders, including two of the most important and sought-after agents in the organisation, one of whom was the legendary 'White Rabbit' (Flight Lieutenant F. F. E. Yeo-Thomas – later Wing Commander – GC,

MC) who had been recalled to London. Arriving in Arras from Paris on 10 November he succeeded in contracting Mrs Fraser at her perfumery but two days later he had to go back to Paris. Returning again to Arras on the 13th he received instructions that, with two women agents, he was to be picked up by a Lysander aircraft at a ground called Charante, twenty miles away. However, a complete German division had just moved into the area through which it would be necessary to travel.

Apart from those periods when Yeo-Thomas was visiting Paris and agents in the Arras area to assess their requirements he was accommodated by Mrs Fraser under considerable risk. Recollecting that there was a graveyard not far from the landing ground, she organised a fake funeral and obtained a closed motor hearse, several undertaker's mutes in full fig, petrol and a coffin. With a suitcase of vital documents concerning the German V1 and V2 weapons concealed in the coffin and Yeo-Thomas as well as the women hidden under flowers in the hearse the journey was completed successfully, enabling them to be picked up on the night of the 15th/16th, then returned to England.

When she could not provide shelter personally for the escapers, evaders (including aircrew) or agents Mrs Fraser arranged to accommodate them with friends. Her numerous hiding places for the immediate storage of weapons and supplies which arrived by parachute included the municipal slaughterhouse and she also provided, at the request of the commander of Zone Nord, valuable intelligence information regarding enemy troop movements and fortifications so that it could be passed to Allied Intelligence.

She also carried out extremely hazardous work as a courier, travelling long distances by car and on foot with compromising documents and, frequently, with arms and explosives needed for important sabotage operations. She collected these supplies from clandestine parachute grounds and stored them in one of her safe houses in Arras, only allowing them to be released on production of a pass signed by herself. During this period her house was used as a meeting place for all the more important Resistance gatherings and conferences in the Arras district. She was betrayed by an agent whom she had sheltered, and re-arrested on 18 February 1944 by the Gestapo, the members of which were determined to extract from her everything that she knew about the Resistance. This determination was opposed by her grim determination not to betray the innumerable patriots that she had met or worked with, in the certain knowledge that she would have to face sustained torture, even death, at the hands of her captors.

She was examined, re-examined and cross-examined mercilessly at Loos during the next twenty-eight weeks but, although publicly stripped of all her clothes in front of the Gestapo troops and flogged, she still gave nothing away even when confronted with other prisoners. Beaten up time and time again, repeatedly threatened with death, tortured and given the cold water treatment for the whole period of her imprisonment in which she was kept in solitary confinement night and day, she remained unshakeable, showing an unbelievable heroism. At the end of August 1944, with the Allies having broken out of Normandy and reached the area of Amiens, the Gestapo, completely unsuccessful in their efforts to break her down, condemned her to death. She now had every reason to believe that her end was imminent since the Gestapo were not in the habit of sparing those whom they had decided should die but, unknown to her, the Allies had entered Arras on 1 September 1944 and she was liberated by them. She was brought to the United Kingdom where she started her long recuperation from severe physical injuries and mental distress which were to continue to exact their toll until she died in Arras in 1956. Mr Fraser had been a prisoner until his repatriation to England in September 1944 and had thus been incarcerated himself during his wife's periods of imprisonment.

She was recommended for the award of the George Cross but, since her activities as 'Sammy' in *Réseau* Sylvestre were such that they could not be recorded at the time and corroborative evidence could not be produced of her bravery, particularly after her re-arrest on 18 February 1944, this could not be approved and the award of the George Medal was published in *London Gazette Supplement* in the remarkably understated terms of 'For special services to the Allied Cause'. Her medal was presented to her in Paris on 3 December 1946 by the British Ambassador to France, The Right Honourable Alfred Duff Cooper, DSO. In addition to the George Medal, Mrs Fraser was decorated by the United States with the Freedom Medal and by France with the Knight of the Legion of Honour, the War Cross with Palm, the Combattant's Cross, the Commemorative Medal World War II and the Medal for Combatant Resistance Volunteers.

Mlle. Laura Leblanc de Choissay, a captain in the French Women's Service (Corps Auxiliaire Féminin) was one of the early members of the Resistance after the French/German armistice, carrying out a number of dangerous missions for an underground intelligence organisation. She entered the forbidden coastal regions of France regularly and, on occasion, delivered important courier messages by swimming out to an Allied ship waiting off shore. This in spite of these regions being the most heavily guarded in France from which much of the civilian population had been excluded. However, because of the demands of this sort of work her health deteriorated so she was compelled to abandon it, becoming instead assistant to the head of a *réseau* (Resistance group) and the overall controller of all Resistance sectors.

She was arrested by the Axis occupation forces in July 1944 while returning from a mission and, as part of her interrogation, was tortured by the Gestapo which gave orders for her to be deported to Germany. Six weeks later she escaped by jumping from a moving train transporting her to a concentration camp. She had already shown great courage and devotion to duty in accomplishing her intelligence work, accepting danger for the whole of the period of Germany occupation. The honorary award of her George Medal was approved on 30 July 1947 but, when arrangements were being made for it to be presented to her, all efforts to trace her were unsuccessful. It remains, therefore, a matter of conjecture whether she chose to sink out of sight for her own ends or whether she was already dead.

In 1941, almost a year after Dunkirk, British servicemen were still at large in Belgium and northern France, hoping to get back to the United Kingdom. Their numbers were being swollen by Belgian and French aspirants seeking to join the fight, while every weekend, shot down airmen were being added to the total of those in hiding. Living, once more in Avenue Émile Verhaeren, Helmet, near Schaerbeek Station in Brussels was young Belgian woman, **Mlle. Andrée de Jongh**, in whose life so far had been two determining factors. Born in 1916, the first, infant years of her life had been spent in the German-occupied capital and the effect of this was reinforced by her consuming admiration for the English nurse, Miss Edith Cavell, executed by the Germans in 1915 for helping British soldiers to escape from captivity. Under these influences this slim, lively, energetic, determined and attractive young woman was, from early in the second enemy occupation, to follow a mission.

Making use of her first-aid training, although a commercial artist, she moved from one hospital to another in Brussels and Bruges, taking note at the time of the presence of British or Belgian wounded as well as noting the location of possible safe houses and reliable friends. After a friend of hers had completed a reconnaissance to the Spanish border and having raised some money, she led an escape party, which, apart from one English woman, consisted entirely of Belgian officers, all the way to that border. In the course of this journey they had to swim across the River Somme to avoid sentries on the bridges. When she reached Anglat, two miles south-west of Nayonne on the Bay of St. Jean-de-Luz, Département Basses Pyrénées, she met **Mme. Elvira de Greef**, a Belgian woman in her mid-forties who, intent upon escaping to England via Bordeaux with her children, had been trapped there in the 1940 holiday season.

Born Elvira Berlement in Brussels on 29 June 1897 she was now slightly built, with a round face and high cheek bones. Her prominent eyes were grey tinged with green and her dark hair was cut short. Her resolute, even ruthless, personality was ideally suited to the role that she was to play. From this time forward Mlle. de Jongh was to be known as ‘Dédée’, the diminutive form of her christian name, and

Miss Andrée de Jongh GM
(photo: Imperial War Museum).

Mme. de Greef would be known as 'Tante Go', a local term of affection based on the name of a well-remembered pet dog.

After returning to her base in the Helmet house Dédée set off with ten young Belgians and Private Cromar Cupar, a Gordon Highlander who had evaded capture at St. Valery-en-Caux and who, a week later, in August 1940, was in the office of the British Consul in Bilbao, northern Spain, a journey of more than seven hundred miles. The Germans, who were eventually to build continuous massive fortifications along the French Atlantic coast (*der Westwall*), had declared a coastal zone into which unauthorised entry was forbidden but, despite this, the journey through Belgium and France was made, almost entirely, by train. The final eight-hour journey across the Pyrenees, however, had to be made on foot using precipitous paths and crossing the River Bidassoa.

Faced with this tiny, simply-dressed twenty-five-year-old who had spent two days travelling through Spain from the mountains, the Consul at Bilbao agreed to represent her case to London to have the escape line (then called 'Postman') recognised and to provide funds for paying the essential Pyrenean guides. Further enthused by this successful trip Dédée reached Bilbao again in October with another small party, to be told that approval had been given for funding the line all the way from Brussels and that the Allies regarded transmission of aircrew as the highest priority. It was also agreed that wireless operators would not be introduced from outside, the line remaining wholly Belgian-controlled and organised. Quite early in the history of the line – which was soon to be renamed 'Comet' – the Gestapo became suspicious of her activities as she had transferred her base to Paris and continued passing 'parcels' from there.

It was necessary to break every journey in a number of places, each pause involving its own quota of risks, but she was totally alert to every situation however difficult, using her initiative and complete *sang-froid*. She would agree with the Germans, forcing them by sheer strength of personality to let through her companion in whatever assumed guise he was travelling. She crossed the Pyrenees in all weathers – snow and ice in mid-winter, rain and summer heat – each journey requiring the

Bidassoa to be crossed although at times it could become a raging torrent. One of her best agents was drowned during a crossing and, on another journey, frontier guards set an ambush in the mountains but, being made aware of the situation, she delayed their departure and, two days later, led her party through safely. On these arduous journeys she not only offered encouragement to her often weakened charges but, when necessary, provided physical support.

In August 1941 her father, M. Frederic Émile de Jongh, the forty-eight-year-old headmaster of a school in Place Goucheret, near Gare du Nord, had started to run the Brussels end of the line (code-name 'Paul') and was totally committed to his daughter's work. In April 1942, he also moved to Paris and continued to operate from there until he was arrested on 6 June 1943 by the Gestapo who subjected him to brutal interrogation. Despite this, and the knowledge that she was being sought constantly by the Germans, Dédée refused to abandon her role. On the contrary, she returned to Brussels several times managing, on one occasion, to escape through her garden after the Gestapo had appeared at the door of her house. Her father was to be executed at Mont-Valerian, a fort occupying the bend of the River Seine in western Paris, on 28 March 1944 without disclosing any secrets and was awarded a posthumous King's Commendation for Brave Conduct.

Arrested near the village of Urrungue on the Franco-Spanish frontier on 15 January 1943 in the company of three airmen evaders, Dédée was lodged in prison at St. Jean-de-Luz, then at Bayonne, Département de Basses-Pyrénées before being transferred, via Biarritz, to the inhuman Fresnes prison on the outskirts of Paris. Her arrest virtually destroyed Comet which had already been the target of infiltration and arrests so Tante Go, who was the organiser of its southern sector, was forced to reduce the frequency of 'movements' but not before she had undertaken an audacious and highly dangerous mission – nothing short of attempting Dédée's rescue from captivity in Bayonne. Regrettably, this failed, but Tante Go's drive and indomitable courage were to reinstate the line which continued to pass much-needed evaders back to the fight.

Assisted, as ever, by her husband Fernand's employment as an interpreter in the German *Kommandatur* at Anglet, where he had access to information, stationery and official stamps, she had from the start been ruthlessly energetic, her activities in the black market being essential for the feeding of her charges. It also enabled her to accumulate information with which to corrupt German sentries and higher officials and, travelling throughout the area every day on her bicycle, meant that she met smugglers, cafe and bistro proprietors and others making possible the lodging of about four hundred airmen in the area and their transfer to Spain. On frequent occasions she conducted them personally towards the frontier and showed even greater bravery by maintaining a long contact with the British representative in Madrid, essential to the continued success of the line. Her practical common sense enabled her to continue successful operations in the face of arrest of important members of the line, flouting every danger and difficulty until the liberation. As a final gesture of defiance in July 1944 she organised and took part in the successful rescue of one of the Pyrenean guides, a giant Basque smuggler, lodged in a civilian hospital in Bayonne, who had been wounded and captured while conveying secret intelligence massages. With her husband she was delivered from danger when the Allies overran their area in July 1944 and they were reunited with their children Freddy and Janine, who had been flown over from England especially. After the war they returned to Belgium where she died in August 1991 in Brussels, her husband having pre-deceased her.

At the time of her arrest Dédée had completed twenty-five journeys in which she had been responsible for conveying 112 men, and had drawn up a five page plan to cover every aspect of the route for the operations. After she had spent some time in Fresnes she was transferred to Brussels where she passed through the hands of the *Lüftwaffe* interrogators into those of the Gestapo before, their efforts to force information out of her having failed, she was shipped to Ravensbrück concentration camp and, finally, to Mauthausen.

Her morale remained unbroken throughout the unspeakable horrors of these camps and, at the latter, when women were ordered to work on removing debris from the railway lines – during which over fifty were reported to have been killed – she protested to the Germans on their behalf. This action brought her three days solitary confinement but she lived to be repatriated, via Switzerland, on 7 May 1945, greatly weakened by her experiences. After recovering from her serious illness she looked after her mother and then undertook nursing training before working as a sister in a leper hospital in the Belgian Congo. When the Congo became independent (as Zaire) she was obliged to leave, the hospital being destroyed later, and she was appointed as matron of a hospital in Addis Ababa, Abyssinia before going to work in Senegal. She lives now in Brussels after a life given unremittingly to the service of others.

During the post-war consideration of awards it was decided that Andrée de Jongh could not be given the George Cross as she was a foreign national and the Royal Warrant specifically excluded such an award but, as a special gesture of appreciation, she would be invested personally by HM The King at Buckingham Palace. Accordingly, she was brought to Northolt airfield in an RAF Dakota on 11 February 1946, accommodated at the Savoy Hotel, then returned to Brussels on the 15th after her investiture on the 13th. To add to this signal honour (until 1982 the only honorary award of the George Medal to be presented at the Palace by the Monarch) she was entertained by the Air Minister and Air Staff and by the Belgian Ambassador with representatives of the United Nations. She was also taken to visit the Tower of London – not exactly an attraction in view of her recent experiences – St. Paul's Cathedral and the House of Commons, then presented with a personal memento in the form of a specially mounted, inscribed clock from an RAF bomber aircraft, symbolic of all the aircrew who had passed down the Comet line.

Mrs Elvira de Greef was recommended, originally, for the MBE but, after reconsideration (337 aircrew had passed through her hands), this was raised to the George Medal with which she was presented by the British Ambassador to Belgium, Sir Montgomery Knatchbull-Huggeson, KCMG early in 1946.

In the Comet northern sector **Mlle. Aline Lily Dumont** started her activities in Brussels shortly after her parents and sister Andrée (Nadine) who were also members had been arrested by the Gestapo in August 1942. Having called herself 'Lily' all her life this was the name by which she was known to all of 'her' airmen. Her work as a liaison agent in different areas was to collect airmen from the whole of Belgium and hand them over to other members of the line who despatched them to Paris. Being known, for reasons of security, by a variety of code names in different areas she was also helping with the forging of identity documents for both evaders and guides so that between two and four airmen were able to leave Brussels for the frontier every two days. However, by June 1943, there had been so many arrests that there was hardly anybody left in the line so she was obliged to move from place to place to avoid arrest herself. No danger, however great, was able to divert her from her work.

Again and again she escorted parties of evaders through German controls at any one of which she might easily have been arrested and subjected to interrogation by the Gestapo. On one occasion, having been arrested, her *sang-froid* managed to trick the Gestapo into releasing her. For more than a year she continued to convey and hide airmen in Belgium but in January 1944, owing to the activities of the German *Feldpolizei* (Field Police), she was told to leave the country as she was now 'blown'. Undaunted, she went to Paris to operate there instead. While there she was followed by a member of the Gestapo but, becoming aware of this, she alerted her companions and they eliminated him so that the line could continue to operate. On 26 February she went to Bayonne then to Madrid and, leaving there on 3 March, returned to Brussels to study the situation and collect information about airmen who were known to have landed on Belgian territory.

She waited there for a few days before going back to Paris to wait for the airmen, conveying them in five parties to the south. While in Paris she was determined to find out who was the traitor who had penetrated the line to create such havoc so she went to Fresnes Prison, standing under its walls at a point from where she could see the women's quarters. She then shouted to a French woman among those taken prisoner, receiving the reply that she needed. The grave risk taken and information received, she fled the scene only to be stopped by a policeman but, assuming the winsomeness of her pretended age – fifteen – she won over the Commandant and was allowed to leave and take the train to Bayonne. The pretence was assisted by the fact that she was only five feet tall, a childlike sturdy figure with a voice to match, slightly built with high cheekbones. She stayed in Anglet with Tante Go helping with the evacuations and reforming the line but it was not until 10 May that she was persuaded (ordered) to return to Madrid from where she was passed, via Gibraltar, to the United Kingdom.

She must have handled, in the course of her astonishing career with the line, more than 250 evaders and her name became a legend among countless airmen shepherded across Brussels by her. In spite of the arrest of her family and being herself imprisoned in Fresnes Prison for two days she continued to pursue those ideals shared by the others who were also awarded the George Medal with which she was presented by Sir Hugh Montgomery Knatchbull-Huggeson, KCMG in early 1946.

The younger of a doctor's two daughters, Lily Dumont was born in May 1921 in Uccle, a southern suburb of Brussels, her mother having been a nurse in the First World War in which her father had been a volunteer. He took up a medical appointment afterwards in the Belgian Congo and in 1927 his wife and daughters joined him there but, as he was practising in the bush, there was no school. The family returned to Belgium in 1932 where Lily attended primary school in Uccle for two years before studying at the Athenée and, in September 1940, started nursing training at University Hospital, St. Pierre in Brussels. Before starting at St. Pierre she had helped wounded evacuees from the eastern border and British soldiers who had been unable to re-embark at the time of Dunkirk. She also helped her parents to hide soldiers and distribute clandestine pamphlets while continuing to help Allied escapers and evaders during her training. She finished training in June 1943 and worked for the underground until forced to leave for Paris in January 1944.

Having been murdered by the Germans her father did not return after the war but her sister Andrée survived Ravensbrück concentration camp, having been held at St. Giles Prison after her arrest. 'Michou' (as she was known) married Capte. Pierre Ugeux, a Belgian officer in the SAS, in August 1945 and they now live near Uzès, Département Gard, southern France, having had four children.

The international aspect of the evaders and escapers with which the line dealt and the territory over which it operated was reflected in the range of other awards that were given to these three outstandingly gallant ladies:

Dédée – By Belgium: War Cross with Palm, Officer of the Order of Leopold II; Medal for Resistance Army 1940–1945; Commemorative Medal with Star between two Crosses, Medal for Political Prisoners with 5 Palms. By France: War Cross; Officer of the Legion of Honour. By the United States: Medal of Freedom with Gold Palm.

Tante Go – by Belgium: War Cross with Palm; Resistance Cross; Officer of the Order of the Crown with Palm; Commemorative Medal with Star between two Crosses. By France: War Cross; Officer of the Legion of Honour. By the United States: Medal of Freedom with Gold Palm.

Michou – by Belgium: War Cross with Palm; Knight of the Order of Leopold II; Knight's Cross of the Order of the Crown with Palm; Medal for the Resistance Army 1940–1945, Commemorative Medal with Stars between Crosses; Combatant Volunteers Medal; Evaders' Cross. By the United States: Medal of Freedom with Palm.

While Berthe Fraser's activities were confined, in the main, to the area of France around Arras and the Comet Line extended southwards from the Brussels region, the same need to convey 'parcels' existed to the north and east. The Netherlands did not attract escapers and evaders connected with the British Expeditionary Force since it was too far north to be on the normal escape routes after Dunkirk. However, two main categories of people in these areas needed to leave the continent – Dutchmen trying to join their government in exile and thus their nascent armed forces, and Allied aircrew on their way to rejoin the fight. There was also a third category consisting of Jews of all ages and both sexes, constantly at risk with the hand of every Nazi and collaborator turned against them. These problems were exacerbated by the flat Dutch terrain which limited the opportunities to move unseen and the presence of so many waterways running across the escape routes.

Miss Johanna Maria Folmer (known everywhere as 'Joke')* was born on 9 July 1923 in Hookddorp in Holland between Amsterdam and Haarlam, her father the administrator of a sugar plantation near Bandung in Java. She spent the first sixteen years of her life in the Dutch East Indies, returning to her homeland in 1939 as a student, first at Zeist near Utrecht and then at the Social Academy in Amsterdam. Having lived under German occupation for two years she started working for the Dutch Resistance in 1942 with her room in the Academy as a base, giving shelter in her parents' house to Jews, students and others hiding from the enemy and guiding French prisoners of war to the Belgian frontier. In 1943 the escape organisation that she was working for, '*Fiat Libertas*' (Let There Be Liberty), formed originally as an intelligence gathering group, turned more and more to helping escapers as that problem became more pressing. She was now travelling all over the Netherlands connecting, on occasions, with the Comet Line. In September 1943, however, the whole organisation was penetrated because a member talked and the Germans started to roll it up from Paris through Brussels to the Netherlands. With numerous arrests being made she stepped into the breach immediately and worked to rebuild the line and, from that time until her arrest in April 1944, she spent her time rescuing numerous evaders at large in the Netherlands. In contact with every important figure and

* Pronounced 'Yoker'.

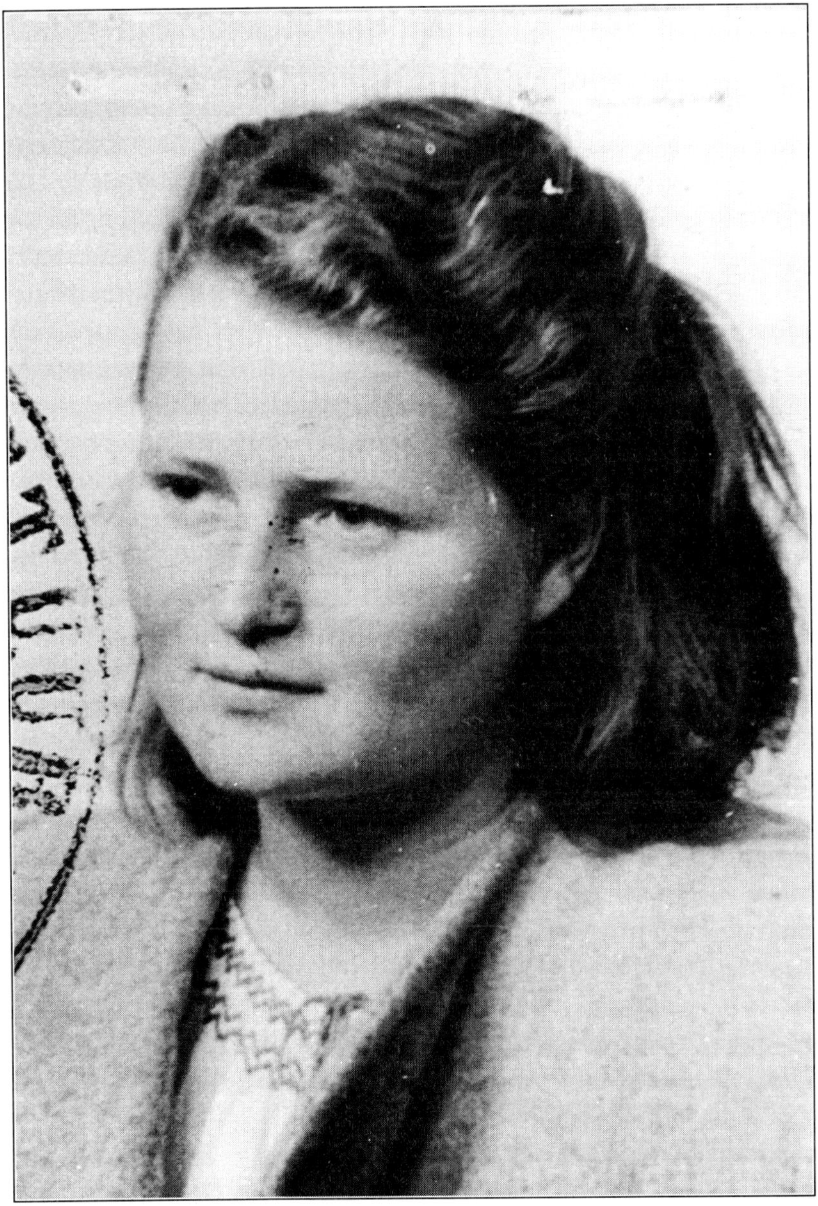

Miss Johanna Maria Folmer GM
(her wartime ID photograph).

organisation in Dutch evasion circles she travelled to all areas where there were men and women awaiting her arrival. Every one of these was conducted, personally, to the southernmost area of the country in Limburg where they were taken over by others for the next stage; but, on eight occasions, she accompanied 'parcels' to Brussels herself.

Throughout the winter of 1943/44 she never spared herself for an instant and was in constant danger while engaged in this vital work. On one journey she escorted, through the whole length of the Netherlands, an escaper who had been in hospital with his face severely burned, hardly able to walk, his description having been circulated throughout the whole country. She also guided an Indian and a Negro evader on separate trips, each presenting unusual difficulties because of appearance. She was arrested in Amsterdam Central Station while meeting her mother for the day together, the Germans having followed Mrs Folmer. The last member of her organisation to be captured, its records had already been burned but she could remember having helped up to a hundred Allied evaders. All reliable estimates, however, agree that she had given personal assistance to approximately three hundred people including French prisoners of war, and had sheltered seventeen evaders, almost all Allied aircrew, in her family's house for periods of up to sixteen days.

This general view is supported by the citation for her American medal which stated that she had helped more than three hundred Allied airmen. She was taken to Scheveningen prison where she was first subjected to six weeks' solitary confinement before being interrogated, after which she was tried and sentenced. She was then passed through Vught concentration camp near s'Hertogenbosch and prisons at Anrath, just over the Dutch/German border, Ziegenham, south-west of Berlin, Cottbus south-east of Berlin, and Waldheim.

Throughout her periods of activity and incarceration she displayed complete fearlessness and unswerving devotion to duty. For one so young to take over in such tragic and dangerous circumstances and then make an outstanding success of the task in a severely controlled country where, all too often, factions tended to work against each other, was an outstanding achievement. After her arrest she was eventually sentenced to death but refused to give any information to the Germans. Her proud bearing secured for her the respect of her captors, even of the Gestapo, and her quiet courage and warm friendship throughout fifteen months of savage treatment in the different prisons were an inspiration to her fellow prisoners.

Liberated by the Russians on Sunday 6 May 1945 her troubles were by no means over although, together with her erstwhile fellow prisoners, she was able to move freely around the camp after eight months in German prisons. Waldheim, in Saxony, was thirty miles west of Dresden, twenty-five miles east of Altenburg and thirty miles north of the Czechoslovakian border, an area fated to spend forty-five years as part of East Germany (DDR). For the first few days the occupants – French, Poles, Dutch, Belgians – left to their own resources, spent their time searching the camp for food, any food! Three Dutch women, Henriette Roosenburg, Joke Folmer and Nell Lind, banded together with F. Driessenter Meulen, a merchant seaman, all under sentence of death as 'politicals', and decided to take their chances as a group. They also took under their wing another Dutch woman 'Fafa' who had been sentenced to death and was crippled with arthritis.

With the arrival of the Russians it became obvious that the official plan was to repatriate them via Dresden and Odessa on the north-west shore of the Black Sea, diametrically opposite to the direction in which they wished to travel. They therefore decided to make their own way through the war-torn countryside, walking initially northwards. Subsisting on food and milk that they could scrounge they passed through the small town of Ostra and stayed overnight at Ragwitz Castle, then carried on to the town of Reisa on the River Elbe, north-west of Dresden, looking for a boat. By good fortune they came upon two Dutch river barges moored at the opposite river bank and unable to proceed because ruined bridges were blocking the river. The barge masters having promised to obtain a boat for them, the four wanderers, with great difficulty, obtained a Russian local pass to avoid incarceration in an official camp. Returning to the barges next day they found a boat waiting for them and were entertained to a magnificent Dutch Whit-Monday lunch with schnapps.

Then, after a deep sleep followed by a huge breakfast they set off towards Mühlberg and Torgau where they negotiated a raging torrent pouring through the twisted steel of a ruined railway bridge. After being royally entertained by a Dutch couple on a barge near the village of Dommitzsh their luck ran out at Wittenburg where the Russians directed them to the displaced persons' camp at Coswig, fifteen miles short of the Americans at Dessau. From 25 May until 6 June they stayed in this dilapidated, vermin-ridden camp, sustained and protected by the Dutch element therein. Then, after more walking, they were ferried across the Elbe to Dessau into the hands of the Red Cross to be faced with an indefinite delay in another camp while waiting for space on a train. They had now travelled almost a hundred miles since Waldheim.

Having established their status as 'politicals' they were able to hitch a lift two days later on an American truck to Halle airfield thirty miles south where they were placed aboard an American Dakota and flown to another airfield near Brussels. Their reception and clearance took three days before they boarded a train at Brussels North station bound for Oudenbosch, North Brabant, still some distance from their respective homes but in their native country at last! They were accommodated in a Roman Catholic monastery where they passed medical and political examinations, then chance took another hand. A fortuitous meeting with a Dutch officer, Henriette's cousin, produced a car on 13 June which took them on a 'secret' mission – a round trip to their homes and, in Zeist, Joke was reunited with her mother to be told that her father and brothers had all survived and were safe.

Her honorary George Medal was approved on 28 July 1947 and presented at the Ridderzall, The Hague by Sir George Nevill Maltby Brand, KCVO, CMG, the British Ambassador to The Netherlands, on 11 December of that year. She was also awarded the Dutch Resistance Cross, the Dutch Bronze Lion Decoration, the French Combattant's Cross and the United States Freedom Medal with Palm.

After the war she returned to the Social Academy where she qualified in juvenile delinquency studies and worked in that field in the three northern Dutch provincial districts until retirement in 1984. Marrying in Zeist in 1950 she is the mother of six children although divorced in 1969. She had also fostered six other children! Her brother died several years ago and her foster brother emigrated to the USA where he served in the USAF. She had lived for the last sixteen years on Schiermonnikoog, a national park and one of the Fresian Islands off the north coast of the Netherlands.

As a preliminary to Operation Overlord (the D-Day landings in Normandy) a joint operation ('Sussex') was mounted in which teams of two or three agents were inserted into France and Belgium in late April and early May 1944. About fifty teams, often of mixed nationality and all in plain clothes, were spread in an arc extending from Brussels to Rennes, Département Ille et Vilaine, France to provide tactical intelligence to Overlord planners. Run jointly by MI6 (UK), the SI Branch of OSS (USA) and Bureau Central de Recherches et d'Action à Londres 'BRAL', the Gaullist headquarters in London, each team was equipped with WT (morse) and RT (voice). In regions tense with impatient anticipation among the population and jumpiness in the occupying forces who could sense defeat, they were, if not detected by the enemy, to remain in position until over-run and picked up by the Allied forces. **Mlle. Jeanette Gauthier**, in fact, parachuted in earlier than the others on 8 February and was the first 'Sussex' agent to jump, acting as principal agent of the operation's four strong Pathfinder Group which, in the interests of security, had been instructed not to contact existing Resistance networks.

They landed in central France near Châteauroux, Département D'Indre, bad weather having delayed the drop which had been carried out without most of their supplies, left behind in error. They found that most of their potential contacts had either moved or been arrested so, with the Allied landings imminent, she decided to ignore the original instructions about existing networks and made reception arrangements with some of them. The group's original directive was to locate suitable parachutages, temporary and permanent hideouts and emergency refuges for radio operators as well as to develop well-placed informants. For seven months they travelled considerable distances covering most of northern France from the Loire to the Belgian border and from the Atlantic coast to Alsace-Lorraine and succeeded in arranging the reception and conveyance to safe houses of many of the 'Sussex' teams. During this long period she exhibited the highest qualities of initiative, daring and endurance, undertaking the most risky assignments herself, her work and conduct being beyond praise.

Unusually for a woman engaged on special duties, she held a commission in the French Army (Corps Auxiliaire Féminin). On 30 October 1947 she was presented with her honorary George Medal by the British Ambassador, The Right Honourable Alfred Duff Cooper, DSO in Paris. All efforts to trace this gallant lady have been unsuccessful.

Chapter 6

Resistance/Underground – Mediterranean and South-East Asia

OTHER George Medals were awarded to women for activities outside north-west Europe, three being for gallantry in the Mediterranean area and one in South-East Asia. One common thread runs through these activities, however: determination to frustrate the evil plans of a pitiless and vicious occupying foreign power, determination taken to the very threshold of death not for hours but for days and weeks extending to the brink of human endurance.

Nancy Wake was born in Wellington, New Zealand on 30 August 1912 but, at the age of two, was taken to Sydney, NSW, Australia by her New Zealander parents. Educated there, she left for Europe, as many young Antipodeans still do, in December 1932 and reached Paris, via Vancouver, New York, Liverpool and, in 1934, a college of journalism in London where she became a free-lance journalist. Based on Paris she travelled throughout France in search of stories and was in Marseilles on 9 October 1934 to witness the assassination of King Alexander of Yugoslavia. During her travels she met Henri Fiocca, a well-to-do businessman, in Juan-les-Pins, a resort in Département Alps-Maritimes and, after her trip back to England, they were married in Paris on 30 November 1939. Her idyllic life of luxury was interrupted by Henri's call to military service at Belfort in Alsace so, after hurried training, she became a rather less than efficient driver of a private improvised ambulance provided by her husband. Having seen service near the Rhine she was ordered back to Paris after which her vehicle broke down at Nîmes so she had to hitch a lift for the last seventy miles to Marseilles.

With France partitioned by the Germans in 1940 she took on the role of supporting British POWs in Fort St. John, buying food and cigarettes for them and entertaining them at her home. After the prisoners had been transferred to Fort St. Hippolyte au Fort she became involved with the 'Pat' escape line in the course of which she organised and helped its second-in-command to escape. She continued to act as an escort even after the Germans occupied the whole of France in November 1942 until the Gestapo's attentions forced her to leave the country. Known to them as 'The White Mouse' she had been actively sought for months.

Having reached the United Kingdom by sea from Gibraltar in June 1943 Madame Nancy Fiocca was commissioned into the First Aid Nursing Yeomanry (FANY) as **Ensign Nancy Grace Augusta Wake**, reverting to her maiden name after offering her services to the Free French Forces who were not interested. On commissioning, she joined SOE in Colonel Buckmaster's group and was committed to a tough, all-embracing series of courses to prepare her for her return to France. She had mixed results on these courses and provided some entertainment to both staff and fellow students. These finished, following a full briefing, she boarded a Liberator aircraft at an airfield in southern England on the night of 29 February 1944 with another agent. The intention was that she should act as assistant, under the name of Mme. Andrée, to a fresh organiser being sent separately in a Lysander aircraft to take over an important circuit, Freelance, in the Auvergne mountains.

The two agents landed by parachute at 1.30 a.m. in a field between Hérisson and Cerilly, north of Montluçon, Département Allier and, having been received successfully, were transported with a large sum of money and the plans to support the 'Second Front' to the village of Cosne-d'Allier, just to the west of Montluçon, where they rested and waited for the organiser to arrive. Four days later, however, news came that he had been arrested with a large number of his group including the radio operator so there was no means of communicating with London. What was more, in the absence of any information, they could not contact 'Gaspard', the chief of the whole area. Not being the most patient of individuals she became edgy and fretful so feelers were put out and pressure brought to bear with the result that, passing through a number of 'cut-outs', they eventually reached the first main contact who made arrangements for the required meeting.

The area in which they were now working was a highland district with mountains up to 2,000 metres, plateaux, jagged volcanic rock formations, heavily wooded slopes and gorges, with the weather mostly cold and wet – the whole area inaccessible. Several days later, more than ninety miles south, they met Gaspard, a most unprepossessing man, at Mont Mouchet, near St. Flour, Département Chaudes-Aignes where she spent several months helping to train and instruct *maquisard* groups. She took part in several engagements against the enemy, showing the utmost bravery under fire. During a German attack after two American officers had been parachuted in to help the *maquis*, the leader of the section of ten men became demoralised so she led them, personally, to within point-blank range of the enemy, directed the fire, rescued the parachutist and withdrew in good order, showing exceptional coolness and courage.

Finding herself in control of more than 7,000 men who had been without a leader since their last one had been killed in a German raid, tough, hard-bitten men who resented a woman giving them orders, she took over by sheer personality. Recognising the serious threat posed by such a force of *maquisards* the Germans reacted with atrocities, ruthless oppression and all the brutality for which they had become infamous. Throwing in 20,000 SS troops with artillery and air support the Germans mounted a full-scale attack on 20 June against the stronghold at Chaudes-Aigues which developed into a pitched battle during which Nancy was everywhere, distributing truck loads of weapons, ammunition and supplies, many of them wrenched from newly arrived parachutages, to the *maquis* positions. Often under heavy fire, she narrowly escaped disaster when the farmhouse in which she was resting was shelled and then, later in the same evening, her car was riddled with machine gun fire from an attacking aircraft. Seconds after she and her young *maquisard* colleague had dived into a ditch, the car exploded in a ball of flame so she completed her mission on foot.

With heavy casualties being suffered on both sides, orders arrived from General König, the senior officer of the Free French Forces in Britain (who was later to liberate Paris), that the Auvergne *maquis* should disengage and revert to the traditional practices of guerrilla warfare. Arriving after three days and nights at a village called Saint Santon, near Aurillac, Département Cantal, bedevilled most of the time by spotter planes, she found that the radio had been hidden and the codes destroyed so that she was out of contact with London. With Allied forces now ashore in Normandy this contact was vital to the Auvergne *maquis*' operational capability, positioned as it was astride the German reinforcement route from southern France but, as far as she could establish, the nearest available radio and operator were located at Châteauroux, two hundred kilometres to the north-north-west.

The final route by which she was forced to travel on foot and bicycle was nearer, in fact, three hundred kilometres long because Châteauroux was under strict Gestapo surveillance, but contact with London being vital, a new radio and codes had to be dropped. After seventy-two hours virtually non-stop movement in mountainous terrain she returned to Saint Santon, saddle-sore, totally exhausted, her legs in agony and with every nerve in her body screaming for relief, a full day ahead of her expected arrival. After recovering from this ordeal she moved northwards to Département Allier in July where, in the neighbourhood of Ygrande, she joined a force of two thousand *maquisards* in ambushing German convoys trying to reach Normandy. Their activities culminated, by the end of August, in the destruction of targets allocated to support the Allied Riviera landings. All except, that is, a small synthetic oil plant in Saint-Hilaire which was taken over, filling the dual purposes of supplying the *maquis* with fuel and denying it to the *Wehrmacht*. She then, with a force of only two hundred, participated in the actions which repulsed the attack of 6,000 Germans and, later, with only fifteen others, raided the Gestapo headquarters in Montluçon, killing thirty-eight Germans.

Promoted captain, Nancy was now going into action wearing full military battle-dress, fighting alongside uniformed *maquisards*. During her period in central France her organising ability, endurance, courage and complete disregard for personal danger earned her the respect and admiration of all, most of them rough and difficult to handle, with whom she came into contact. They accepted her orders and treated her as one of their own male officers.

Her satisfaction after the August 1944 success at Montluçon was totally destroyed by the devastating news that Henri Fiocca had been captured by the Gestapo on 16 October 1943 and, after the foulest torture, executed in September 1944. Returning to England in October she contacted Colonel Buckmaster and then, some time later, went back to Marseille where she remained until the German surrender. Paris followed, then the London Victory parade and, in 1947, Prague. In 1948, in Paris she was invested with the George Medal by the British Ambassador, Sir Oliver Charles Harvey, GCMG, CB on 21 April. She was also invested with the United States Medal of Freedom with Bronze Palm, two French War Crosses with Palm, another with Star and the Resistance Medal. In 1949 she went back to Sydney where she stood, unsuccessfully, for the Federal Parliament but reduced the Liberal candidate's majority to almost nothing. In 1957 in England she married John Forward whom she had met in Malta and, after a time, they returned finally to Australia where they live in New South Wales but still travel extensively.

Italy, in its role as Axis jackal, scavenging for scraps left by stronger and braver predators, attacked Greece through Albania on 1 November 1940 and was repulsed immediately. Il Duce's subsequent record against the Greeks was so abysmal that his Axis partner was forced to take a hand so the German forces drove south through the Balkans.

With the RAF already in Greece and the Germans nearing the northern border, British land forces, scraped together from within the Middle East, honoured the British Government's rash pledge to the Greek monarch and landed in support of his army. Five weeks later the Allied forces had been driven out of Greece and three weeks after that, on 2 May 1941, out of Crete. This unwise decision made our situation in the Middle East extremely precarious and resulted in very great naval losses but gave rise to deep-seated feelings of support among the Greek people. The future of Greece, now occupied by the Germans, was to be one of oppression, hunger and slavery but not surrender.

In September 1943 **Miss Sylvia Apostolides**, the nineteen-year-old daughter of a Greek doctor and his British wife, volunteered to go to the mountains with a British mission. She was told that she would be of greater help if she remained in Athens so she agreed to stay in any capacity. She was first placed in charge of administration of a group of agents employed in collecting information about German-controlled airfields, paying their weekly salaries, receiving all their reports and collating them prior to forwarding them to HQ. Most of her work was carried out in her father's surgery so all of her family was in constant danger and, to add to this, she also received and stored consignments of ammunition which, invariably, she transported through the city by taxi. On several occasions she had narrow escapes from capture by the Germans, being fired on once at an enemy road block, and was arrested twice by Greek police.

In addition she played a considerable part in evacuating Allied military personnel, and on one occasion succeeded in conveying some soldiers from the village of Kioura where they had been hiding, through Athens and on to a caique, a small sailing vessel, borrowing the German Admiral's car on the way. She had been arrested first in February 1942 with her mother but succeeded, by judicious bribery, in obtaining their release after a few months. In all of her activities, each involving her in increasing personal danger, she proved to be a most reliable assistant. In the early summer of 1944, the Germans picked up her track again, arresting her with her mother and father early on the morning of 24 June. Subjected immediately to a brutal twenty-four hour interrogation culminating in a savage beating she refused to submit and, after a further three months' incarceration, marked by frequent examination and third degree of every kind, she was condemned to death. Ordered to be executed with eight other girls, in spite of this treatment and the threat of imminent death, she still refused to disclose the name of even one of the members of the mission or their activities.

She was taken out to face the firing squad in the courtyard with the other eight girls but, withdrawing her at the last moment, the Gestapo forced her to witness the others' executions before returning her to her cell. Whatever the reason for this charade she was set free, eventually, with her parents on 23 September 1944. She was presented with her medal (which had been approved on 20 September 1948) by the British Ambassador, Sir Clifford John Norton, KCMG, CVO in Athens on 6 April 1949. By the date of approval she had married, becoming Mrs Sylvia Ioannidou. Widespread enquiries have been made to trace her subsequent history but without success; opinions have been advanced that she left Greece and is now dead.

Born in 1915, the daughter of Count Jerzy Skarbeck and Stephanie (née Goldfeder), Maria Krystyna Skarbeck had an elder brother. In her childhood and youth the free spirit which is part of the Polish character made her a tomboy, vital, healthy but easily bored. On 2 November 1938 she married Jerzy Gyzicki in Warsaw, her previous youthful marriage to Charles Getlich having been dissolved. With Poland defeated in September 1939 and occupied by a ruthless enemy, many Polish men and women were determined to escape from bondage and continue the fight in other campaigns. Maria assumed the role of guide escorting them across the Carpathian Mountains, showing indomitable courage and stamina in the face of great danger. Tall and slender with luxuriant dark hair, she was very brave and intensely patriotic and whole-hearted in her support of the Allied cause.

Having been warned that the Gestapo were looking for her, she made her way through Rumania, Turkey and Syria into the Middle East accompanied by a man, Kennedy, who was to be her romantic companion for a long time. Although having reported to Allied authorities she could not obtain any significant employment suitable to her talents owing largely to an unaccountably vicious campaign that was mounted against her and Kennedy by the Polish Deuxième Bureau. Having previously assumed the name of **Mary Christine Granville** (and been given a British passport in that name) she was given a honorary commission in the Womens' Auxiliary Air Force (WAAF).

With Allied forces back in North-West Europe and the landing in the Riviera yet to take place she parachuted into the Drôme Valley, east of the River Rhône, on the night of 6/7 July 1944, the first SOE woman to be dispatched from Algiers. She was to take up duties as liaison officer to the British Field Officer (Major F. C. A. Cammaerts – 'Roger') working with the *maquis*. Because of her exceptional ability with languages and her previous experience she was also committed to the subversion of satellite troops in the German army and started work straight away. Within a week her success with the Polish troops was so great that, on 17 July, it was regarded as essential that another officer be sent in to help her.

The Normandy invasion having taken place, she remained in the Vercors, a great natural rock formation south-east of Grenoble, an area straddling the Départements of Drôme and Isère, thirty miles by twelve, at an altitude of between 900 and 1,500 metres. Thousands of *maquisards* in three main organisations had made their bases there and their diversionary operations became so unsettling to the occupying forces that the Germans reacted by mounting a massive assault supported by artillery, mortars and aircraft. Despite fierce resistance it became obvious that the *maquis* would be defeated so she was ordered to escape with Roger in the direction of Seyne-les-Alpes, Départment Basses-Alpes. From there she was sent to the Italian frontier where, in spite of previous efforts having failed, she managed to effect a personal liaison with Colonel Marzzalini of the Italian *maquis*.

She then penetrated into Italy across the Alps where she persuaded hundreds of Russians from the *Ost* Legion of the Wermacht to desert and join the local Resistance forces. After then she was arrested twice but, by consummate acting, convinced her captors on each occasion that she was not worth investigating. On another occasion she put her captors in such fear of their lives that they withdrew. Continuing her activities in this area she spent one and a half days climbing through larch forests in the Alps to the 600 metre high Col de Larche where she convinced the Polish garrison to desert the Germans for the Resistance, with the result that they blew up the road and blocked the col.

On 13 August, while travelling from Apt, Département Vaucluse, to Seyne, Département Basses-Alpes, Roger, his second in command, Major Xan Fielding, Commandant Sorrensen and a driver were arrested by the Gestapo and taken to prison at Dignes where the driver was released. Miss Granville ('Pauline') took over all of the mission's work until Roger's successor arrived, then put him in touch with the necessary contacts. In the same period she went to Digne Prison where she posed as Roger's wife and contacted Captain Albert Schenk, the Gestapo liaison officer. Interviewed by all the Gestapo officers except one (a total of eight, all armed) she succeeded over a period of three hours, using a series of amazing stories, threats and bribes, in convincing the Gestapo interpreter, Max Waen, that the three men should be released. The imminence of the Riviera landings was also used as a bargaining point and, after payment of a large ransom, Waen and Schenk, with their wives, escorted the prisoners, twelve hours before they were due to be executed, to Seyne on 17 August. Schenk was killed next day on his return to Digne.

All Miss Granville's activities since she had parachuted in during July had been undertaken in the knowledge that the Yalta conference had already taken place and that her beloved country had been sold out to the Russians but, despite the certainty that she could never return and would be deprived of everything that she held dear, she did not slacken her efforts in the fight against the occupying forces that were ravaging Europe.

Having completed her missions she reported, with Roger, to regional headquarters at Avignon from where she made her way to London but nobody was there to greet her officially and she was left, without money, to her own devices. Although she had been engaged in underground activities against the Axis Powers from soon after the enslavement of Poland until the end of the war in Europe, the George Medal that she was awarded on 1 January 1945 was to mark her multifarious operations in July and August of 1944. Demobilised on 11 November 1945, she was awarded the French War Cross with Silver Star by General Henri Zeller on the 30th of that month for saving Commandant Sorrensen at Dinge.

Abandoned, discreditably, by the Polish and British governments and the SOE, she was too proud to accept any work offered in connection with her wartime activities and her insecurity led to depression which resulted in her going to the south of France. Unsettled, she returned to London where she took a succession of menial jobs before, on 23 November 1946, she received notifications of the grant of British nationality in the name of Christine Granville. She had been given a British passport in Budapest in February 1941 but this was merely an expedient act which did not confer British nationality. Armed with her naturalisation papers she went to Geneva only to be told by a prospective employer, 'You're not British, you're just a foreigner who has managed to get a British passport!'

Totally devastated and demoralised by this knock-out blow she went to Kenya but could not obtain permission to reside there and, when notified that the OBE (Civil) which had been gazetted on 20 May 1947 in the name of Miss Christine Granville 'For special services during military operations prior to 8th May 1945' was to be presented to her with the GM on 20 July 1947 by the governor of Kenya, Major General Sir Philip Euen Mitchell, GCMG, MC, she declined to accept them. This reaction was understandable but, after persuasion by the senior RAF officer in Kenya, she finally agreed.

She eventually took a job as a stewardess in the Shaw Savill Line and served on the liners *Ruahine* and *New Australia* and the Union

Castle's *Winchester Castle*. On the first of these she became friendly with a steward named Dennis George Muldowney who, in a fit of jealousy, stabbed her to death in the Shellbourne Hotel, Kensington on 15 June 1952. She was buried in Kensal Green Catholic Cemetery six days later and her murderer, having been convicted, was hanged on 30 November 1952 in Pentonville Prison. This was a savagely tragic end to a life filled with danger and narrow escapes together with disappointments from people that she thought she could trust. The 'lovely, fragile, small-boned, delicately made, kind and intelligent woman who hated hurting other people' yet was given to icy rages when she sensed injustice, was no more.

More than two years after the outbreak of war, the end of the first week in December 1941 saw shattering successes by the Japanese in their bid for supremacy in the Pacific and Asia. As part of their ambition to create a 'South-East Asia Co-Prosperity Sphere' attacks were mounted, almost simultaneously, on Pearl Harbour (the American base in the Hawaiian Islands), Hong Kong and northern Malaya where the Japanese army landed over the beaches at Khota Baru, Kelantan State, just south of the Siamese border, shortly after midnight local time, 7/8 December. On the 10th, disaster struck when the British battle-cruiser *Repulse* and the battleship *Prince of Wales* were sunk with heavy casualties in air attacks off the east coast of Pahang State. By the beginning of January the Japanese had crossed the northern mountain range, driving defenders southwards to the accompaniment of incessant air-raids to reach Ipoh, Perak State, a growing town on the Kinta River, centre of the tin mining district, 160 miles south-west of the landings.

The speed of the Japanese advance, their utterly ruthless prosecution of the war against military and civilian alike and the difficulties presented by the jungle-clad terrain threw the defenders into disarray, the lack of roads forcing units to pull back from their positions to avoid encirclement. Both **Mrs Sybil Medan Kathigasu** ('Sybil' only in *London Gazette Supplement*), a nurse and midwife, and her husband Dr Adnan Canathapilla (Ziew) Kathigasu, who was in practice in Brewster

Road in the Ipoh suburbs, were members of the Medical Auxiliary Service and she helped most of their neighbours to get away from the bombed areas. Born on 3 September 1899 in Medan, Sumatra, a Eurasian baby girl with three brothers, Sybil Medan Daly was educated in a convent school in Kuala Lumpur in what was the Federated Malay States. As she grew older she qualified in nursing and midwifery in Kuala Lumpur General Hospital, then, on 1 January 1919, she married Dr Kathigasu in the city's Roman Catholic Church of St. John.

Two years later she gave birth to a daughter, Olga, then William Giles Pillay was adopted – he had been born in Rawang, Selangor. A deeply religious woman, Sybil's faith was to sustain her throughout her life both in her work as a nurse supporting her husband and while undergoing the seemingly endless barbarities of the Japanese. A diminutive figure with an incredible strength of character and bubbling personality, she extended every care to others without regarding her personal circumstances.

The doctor having sustained a serious leg wound, she arranged for him to be taken to the hospital where, under operation, a large bomb fragment was removed from his groin. Evacuation ahead of the pitiless invaders becoming inevitable and their adopted son William having been called to arms with the 1st Perak Battalion to end up with the FMS Volunteer Forces in Singapore, they chose to go to Papan, a small town eight miles away between Ipoh and Batu Gajah for no special reason other than that it was situated a little distance from the main Ipoh road and close to the hills of the Kladang Range.

The shock tactics employed by the Japanese in their highly mobile warfare with the bicycle as their basic transport, together with their aerial attacks on main roads, resulted in individuals and small groups of army and air force personnel (British, Australian, Indian and local) becoming separated from the remnants of any parent units or formations. More than twenty of these 'orphans', deciding against retreat, had come together in the area of Papan and joined a guerrilla band (increasingly Chinese communist) in raiding enemy convoys, blowing up bridges and interrupting communications. Problems experienced

Mrs Sybil Kathigasu GM
(photo: Straits Times, *Singapore).*

by evaders everywhere were magnified in Malaya by the external differences between Europeans and the indigenous population, Malay, Chinese and Indian, these limiting the opportunities for merging into or regular contact with the local scene.

The Kathigasus continued to minister to the sick in the area and were contacted by these guerrillas, initially for the treatment of disease, then for the provision of food and medicine and doctoring of wounds as well as for passing information enabling Japanese scouting parties to be avoided in what was later to become a base for the Anti-Japanese Resistance army in the area of Chemor north of Ipoh. With the fall of Singapore on 15 February 1942 the Japanese hold on Malaya, politically, militarily and commercially, became absolute but the Chemor band continued to harass the enemy. During nearly a year from mid-1942 that the guerrillas had been hiding, Sybil's participation had gradually increased, not least by the maintenance of a clandestine news service using a hidden radio. She had also acquired a knowledge of secret hiding places. On 1 August, however, having been betrayed by a Chinese houseboy, she was arrested in her house by the local police and taken to the Central Police Station where the doctor was already under arrest.

Her elder daughter, Olga, was allowed to remain in Papan but William was engaged in helping in the doctor's dispensary. Lodged in Ipoh, Sybil spent a week in the hands of the detective branch (*Toko*) but was then handed over to the Japanese Secret Police, the *Kempetei*, for interrogation. She spent three months under torture, charged with

– Acting as a spy on behalf of and in co-operation with enemy agents in Malaya;
– giving medical attention and other assistance to the communist guerrillas;
– possessing a radio, listening to enemy broadcasts and disseminating enemy propaganda (with ideological differences submerged it was accepted that the Malayan Communist Army was the main Resistance organisation and it was regarded as such by the Japanese).

The *Kempetei* subjected her to every form of torture in a vain effort to compel her to divulge all that she knew about the guerrillas. She was punched, slapped, beaten with sticks and heavy rattan canes, every assault being deliberately localised – so that no nerve or vital organ was permanently damaged – on the outer surface of the upper arm, the thigh and the calf specifically. These areas soon became solid bruises so that she could not lie down and sleep in any sort of comfort. Then, as a change of tactics occasionally, the water torture was used. Eventually, her whole body was reduced to one great throbbing pain but, even though she shouted and screamed at the top of her voice, no information of any interest to the enemy was dragged out of her.

Part way through her interrogation Mrs Kathigasu was moved to *Kempetei* headquarters in Gopeng Road on the outskirts of Ipoh. On 17 November, her five-year-old daughter, Dawn, was brought to the HQ (where her mother was once again undergoing heavy interrogation) to an open space with a tree nearby. After tying Sybil to one of the pillars of a summer house, the *Kempetei* tied Dawn's hands behind her, then suspended her, head down, from a tree the ants in which caused her extreme discomfort. Setting up a brazier beneath her they started to lower her towards the flames, intending to force her mother to divulge the information that the Japanese sought so desperately. As she was about to submit a passing Japanese officer intervened, bringing the incident to a close, and Dawn taken away to safety. Continuing the interrogation, Sergeant Yoshimura knocked Sybil to the ground in frustration and kicked her savagely, damaging her jaw – an injury which was later to cause her great pain – then, on the next day, she was forced to watch her husband being beaten before he was suspended from a tree with his toes just touching the ground and his hands tied behind his back on the rope.

After several more days of unremitting questioning, at the end of a session of being beaten with a cane, Sergeant Yoshimura seized a heavy wooden bar and beat her about the neck and shoulders, striking her squarely on the spine with great force. She fell to the floor in a dead faint and on the following day there was no strength left in her legs and an intense pain racked her body: her response to this was to recite a litany of every Allied success that she could recall from listening to the clandestine radio – after which she fainted clean away. At the end of a month at Gopeng Road she was transferred to Batu Gajah Jail, twelve miles south of Ipoh, where she was scheduled to be put on trial for her life in the Supreme Court. She was so badly crippled by the spinal injury, however, that it was decided that her trial would take place in Batu Gajah Jail on the afternoon of 23 February 1944.

After this travesty had taken place she was sentenced to imprisonment for life but her attitude continued to be one of outright defiance, refusing absolutely on the grounds of conscience to knit puttees and socks for Japanese soldiers serving in Burma, so she was confined in the condemned cell on a meagre diet. Showing great fortitude and patriotism, she persisted in maintaining silence in the face of the Japanese demands right up to the date that she was released by British forces on 2 September 1945 and transferred to Batu Gajah Hospital. The Japanese Government had capitulated on 15 August so the Malayan People's Anti-Japanese Army took charge until the arrival of the British in the shape of two officers of the Special Operations Executive (Force 136).

A period of more than two years had elapsed since Sybil's arrest, with the last two and a half weeks made bearable by reunions with her husband and children but not her much-loved mother who had died in January. The whole town of Papan turned out on her return and a spontaneous collection then raised a large sum of money for her. When she was medically examined after liberation her physical condition was found to be sickening – cracked skull, fractured jaw, and spine so damaged that her legs were paralysed – so, under government auspices, she was flown to England, via Papan, in October 1946 exactly as if wounded in battle.

She was admitted to Boscombe Hospital in Bournemouth where, for two years, doctors fought through ten surgical and plastic operations to restore her health. The *London Gazette Supplement* on 14 October 1947 that published her George Medal also notified the award of the

MBE for her husband Ziew in recognition of his experiences. Sybil Kathigasu was invested with her medal by HM The King at Buckingham Place on 11 November of that year. Dawn was presented with the Malayan Government Commendation for Courageous Conduct during the Occupation.

Succeeding in her ambition to walk unaided and fulfilling a vow that she had made in prison, she made a pilgrimage to Lourdes – to someone with her depth of religious faith a totally fulfilling experience in which she gave thanks for deliverance. Yoshimura, who had been tried and executed in February 1946, was to reach out of the grave however for, while staying in Scotland, she had to be admitted to St. Mary's Hospital, Lanark where she died on 12 June 1948 from septicaemia resulting from her fractured jaw and its neglect. She was buried three days later in the cemetery of St. Mary's Roman Catholic church, Lanark, the ceremony attended by one of the army officers who had released her in Malaya.

Moves were soon in hand to return her body to her own country and later, in January 1949, she was disinterred and taken, by sea in MV *Astynax*, back to her beloved Malaya where, in both Panang and Ipoh, crowds of all races lined the streets in March of that year as a tribute to her memory. She now lies in St. Michael's Church Cemetery, Ipoh where she was joined by her beloved Ziew in December 1972. In the vast numbers populating what was called the British Empire there were, supposedly superior, people who regarded non-white members as not worthy of consideration and such people could never be expected to understand Sybil Kathigasu's patriotism and regard for a federation that did not even enjoy the status of a crown colony let alone a dominion. For her, and more people than it is fashionable to admit today, it was enough to be British and this, allied to her unshakeable religious beliefs, inspired her family and others to follow her remarkable, imperishable example.

Chapter 7

The Fight against Crime

A NOT infrequent feature of the fight against crime, particularly where offences against the person are concerned, involves saving or trying to save human life, and resistance on the part of individuals to crimes of this type give rise to all of the actions for which women were awarded the George Medal. These actions were deliberate, the individuals concerned feeling an inner compulsion in the circumstances to act even after counting the personal risks involved.

The county of Devon has historical standing as the birthplace of many famous seamen such as Drake, Grenville, Hawkins and Raleigh, a tradition perpetuated today, as far as the sea is concerned, by her fishermen and continuing naval associations. Away from the sea, however, it is primarily an agricultural county known for its distinctive red soil and **Miss Marjorie Vearnecombe** came from a farming family. Born to John and Elizabeth Ann Vearnecombe at Chilton Farm, Bickleigh near Tiverton on 17 May 1923, one of five daughters and one son, she went to Cadbury and Cheriton Fitzpaine schools near Crediton. After leaving school she went to live with an aunt and uncle, Mr and Mrs John Greenslade, at Manley Farm near Tiverton and later moved with them to Lutworthy Farm, West Worlington, a small village eleven miles west of that town, where they raised poultry. The farmhouse was divided into two separate dwellings with a communicating door.

The other part was occupied by Mr Frank Percival Webber and his wife Lily who had, up to two years before, lived at Nether Worlington

Farm. Mr Webber had for thirty years been organist at East and West Worlington Churches.

On Friday 22 June 1951, a very fine day, just after 7 a.m., Marjorie, who was upstairs in her room, heard screams coming from the other part of the house. Calling to her aunt and uncle who, on checking, found the connecting door to be locked, she did not pause to don any footwear but ran outside and into the other part of the house by the back door. Upstairs she found fifty-nine-year-old Mr Webber struggling with his wife, who had a cut on her forehead, for possession of a double-barrelled shotgun.

Correctly divining the man's intention to be to injure either himself or his wife, or both, Miss Vearnecombe tackled him immediately and tried to wrench the gun away. Two or three minutes were spent in a violent struggle before the man, who had for some weeks previously been receiving medical treatment, pulled back one of the gun's hammers and pressed the trigger. Unfortunately, at the instant that the gun fired, her right hand was positioned over the muzzle and the top joint of her forefinger was badly injured.

Meanwhile, helped by seventy-five-year-old Mr Greenslade and his wife, Mrs Webber escaped through the back door to take refuge in their part of the house with their door locked. The assailant, exerting all his manic strength, succeeded in breaking free and regaining possession of his gun so, after he had shattered a large pane of glass in a window on their side of the house, the two elderly rescuers and Mrs Webber made for safety in the front part. As Mr Greenslade left by the front door to summon help Mr Webber fired the other barrel, wounding his wife in the head so seriously that she fell to the floor. With Mr Greenslade continuing on his way to a neighbour's house, the sound of another shot was heard from the gunman's part of the house where he was found later to have committed suicide in the kitchen. The telephone party line shared by Lutworthy and the neighbouring property was found to be out of order so Mr Greenslade had to go even further to Worlington, a mile and a half away, before he could summon the police who responded very quickly.

Mrs Webber, who was suffering from severe head injuries, was removed to Tiverton and District General Hospital and, later, to Frenchay Hospital in Bristol where she spent several weeks, her life having been saved, undoubtedly, by Miss Vearnecombe's intervention. Marjorie spent a week in Tiverton Hospital where the top joint of her finger was amputated. She was invested with her George Medal by HRH The Duke of Gloucester at Buckingham Palace on 7 November 1951 and the Carnegie Hero Fund Trust awarded its certificate and £25 on 24 January 1952.

When she left the hospital she returned to the farm, remaining to look after her aunt when her uncle died in February 1953. In March 1988 she left Lutworthy for the last time and now lives in Tidcombe, Devon.

Twelve and a half lines in a *London Gazette Supplement* served to give a brief and arid description of several acts of cold, calculating gallantry displayed by two women police officers in Croydon, Surrey as part of a plan to capture a vicious criminal. November 1954 saw the start of a series of savage attacks on women in Fairfield Path, running between Stanhope Road and Chichester Road, a series which extended throughout the winter. This narrow, almost totally unlit path, twisting for 600 yards with a brick wall running along its west side and trees down the other, lay along the edge of a recreation ground near the centre of the town. Several attacks had taken place when, on 7 March 1955, **Woman Police Constable (WPC) Kathleen Flora Parrott**, in civilian clothes, going off duty at 10.30 p.m., was using the path as a quick way home. Nearing the Chichester Road end, preoccupied, she was attacked by a tall man, aged twenty-eight to thirty, who put his hand on her shoulder. She screamed but the man's arm encircled her neck, tightening to a stranglehold as he forced her to her knees.

Striking out blindly through a red haze she summoned her last reserves of strength and clawed at the mask covering the lower half of the man's face, getting one look at him just before she lost consciousness. The attack had extended through two terror-packed minutes but her screams had been heard so her attacker disappeared, leaving behind the image of his face indelibly printed upon her trained policewoman's memory. Trained in self-defence, she nevertheless sustained injuries to her left knee, right thigh and face, with severe bruising to both sides of her neck caused by the man's grip.

After hospital treatment she had to spend five weeks' convalescing, much of it confined to bed. Returning to duty, she found that although the attacks had been suspended a major police operation had been mounted. Many volunteers were needed as the path was more than a mile from the police station but there had been no shortage of men and women coming forward.

At 7.30 p.m. on Saturday 23 April **Woman Police Sergeant (WPS) Ethel Violet Bush**, with a WPC, both in uniform, was on routine police patrol along the footpath when they saw a man lurking in the bushes trying to make himself even more inconspicuous. Shortly afterwards WPC Parrott, on plain clothes patrol once again, also sighted the man so, covered by two uniformed policemen, she walked along the path to check whether he was the one concerned previously on 7 March but he had disappeared. Meanwhile, WPS Bush had returned to Croydon Police Station in Fell Road where, volunteering, she had changed into plain clothes to lure the man into overt action and so bring about his arrest. Shortly after 9 p.m., as WPS Bush entered Fairfield Path from Stanhope Road acting as a main decoy, the man was seen to leave the recreation ground and start following her. With six policemen posted in strategic positions along the path, WPC Parrott was there too and, as the man passed her position, confirmed by the light of a lamp beside the path that he was the man who had attacked her in March.

With the trap laid, WPS Bush continued the patrol despite her apprehension. She then saw, out of the corner of her eye, the shape of a man following her, keeping to the shadows of the recreation ground. Stretching her courage to the utmost, fighting to keep her eyes to the front, she did not slacken her pace or give any indication although she could see the man catching up with her. Within a couple of paces of her back, before she could turn, he stopped, picked up a Y-shaped piece of yew tree and, using both hands, smashed it down with all his strength on the back of her head. Although softened by the felt hat that she was wearing the blow was severe but, even so, she turned and grasped his jacket lapel, wrestling with him so that the policemen could come up with her. Her plan was frustrated when she was felled by a blow from the man's fist and, in jumping over a glass-topped wall from concealment, the police dog-handler's forearm was ripped open. In a moment of black comedy, he landed on his animal, injuring it, the assailant escaping as a result.

Priority, of course, was given to attending to the WPS and she was removed to Croydon General Hospital where she was found to have a fractured skull and a Y-shaped laceration at the back of her head which needed eleven stitches. Later that night, at a CID conference at Croydon Police Station, WPC Parrott's description caused suspicion to fall on a man who was already well known to the police – a twenty-nine-year-old labourer, 5′10″ tall. He was arrested later at his home and, having initially denied committing the offences, changed his plea after he had been charged. Later, at the Old Bailey (Central Criminal Court), he was sentenced to ten years' imprisonment, it having been decided that he had not been suffering from diminished responsibility. Each policewoman received a contribution from Bow Street Police Reward Fund after the trial and went on to receive their respective medals from HM The Queen at Buckingham Palace on 22 November 1955. In addition to his assault on the policewomen he had been charged and convicted on three previous occasions with attacks on a total of six women. After he was discharged from prison, and as a measure of the danger that he presented to the public, he was once more, in March 1972, sent to prison for raping a fifty-one-year-old woman in Croydon.

Not starry-eyed probationers, fresh out of training school and dashing into trouble blindly, these two ladies, both thirty-nine-year-olds, were mature police officers who, coolly and calmly, volunteered to accept grave personal risk as part of their duty to the public.

WPC Parrott had been born in West Norwood on 10 October 1916

WPS Ethel Violet Bush GM;
WPC Kathleen Flora Parrott GM, Metropolitan Police
(photo: The Associated Press Ltd.).

and went to Benhilton Church School in Sutton and Penwortham Demonstration School in Streatham, south London. She joined the Metropolitan Police on 10 September 1951, all of her service after training being given on the division based on Croydon, receiving another commendation for acting as a decoy. At the time of the incidents she had a ten-year-old son and is now a grandmother living in Croydon. Although passing the sergeants' examination in January 1951 she left in September 1956 for family reasons and went to work in Education Welfare in Croydon.

Born in London in 1916, WPS Bush was one of five children and went to an elementary school then to a trade school in the West End where she learned dressmaking. She joined the Metropolitan Police in 1946 having already served in the Women's Auxiliary Air Force (WAAF) in England, Wales, Northern Ireland and Bombay. In the police she served on divisions in central and east London, south-east London and south of the river as well as on the Croydon division, being promoted to sergeant in 1953 and retiring in 1971. She lives, still single, in Thornton Heath with her sister.

The 330 islands and islets comprising the Fiji group lie in the southern Pacific Ocean, 1,350 miles north of the Bay of Plenty, North Island, New Zealand where the Melanesian and Polynesian cultures meet. The largest of the more than 100 inhabited islands is Vitu Livu in the western part of the group which today is an independent republic but which in 1958 was still a British colony. **Mrs Edith Gladys Collins**, a nursing sister and widow, lived at Suva Point, Laucula Bay near the capital, Suva, on Vitu Livu with her four children. About midnight on 9/10 May 1958, she was awakened by an unusual noise. Getting out of bed, she went to her housegirl's room to find a Fijian man – the girl's husband – standing with an axe in his hands. He smashed this down on the sleeping girl's skull so, completely disregarding her own danger, Mrs Collins rushed at him and tried to wrest the weapon away and was severely injured in the struggle.

Still retaining possession of the axe the man struck his wife again with it, Mrs Collins being knocked down once more while continuing her struggle with him. Then, one of her children having come into the room, she hurried to the child's protection and pushed her from the room. While doing so the nurse sustained further injuries and the twenty-six-year-old man, Jioji Sakaraia Malodali, escaped from the house. He hurled himself over the fence onto a high tension electrical transformer sustaining severe burns and causing two periods of power failure. Police help arrived after 2 a.m. so he was arrested and taken to hospital. Mrs Collins and the housegirl, Akanasi Nasiga, were taken to the Colonial War Memorial Hospital where, sadly, the girl died after admission. The injuries to the nurse's right arm having been dealt with she left the hospital after some days because her young family needed her to care for them.

The assailant was placed under formal arrest, charged and then, on 6 June 1958, tried, convicted and sentenced to death. Having waited in Fiji to give her evidence Mrs Collins returned to Canada where she received her George Medal at the hands of HM The Queen in Ottawa on 1 July 1959.

During the bitterly cold, windy afternoon of 4 March 1964 a desperate lonely man in his twenties was seen holding an infant over sixty feet up on the roof of a three-storey building in Coram Street, off Woburn Place, Holborn in London. Attempts by male police officers to talk him down or seize him were unsuccessful so a call was made to their station at Gray's Inn Road for the assistance of a female officer as being more likely to establish a rapport with him. **Woman Police Constable (WPC) Margaret Shaw Cleland**, who had just come on duty, took the call and, on arrival at the scene, saw that the man, his eighteen-month-old son held firmly in his arms, was sitting on the roof edge with his legs through an iron balustrade. A safety net was rigged below by the fire brigade so, climbing the internal staircase, she gained access to the roof which she found to be a normal pitched one with a low wall, topped by the balustrade, running around its periphery. She had had just three and a half years in the force and had no head for heights but nevertheless, she edged inside the wall along a gulley towards him.

When she reached a spot six feet away from him, he threatened to jump with the little boy so, numbed with cold by this time, she started a conversation. Calmly, talking in an undramatic way, she held his attention, learning that he came originally from Tollcross in east Glasgow about eight miles from her home. She assumed an even broader accent to talk about Scotland, pretending that she knew his home district. Under the fixed, long-range stare of television and press cameras she spoke soothingly, finding out, among other things, that he now lived in Cambridge and had decided on this line of action whilst in a fit of depression. Before setting out he had rung up newspapers announcing his intention which was the reason for the saturation media coverage that the incident was attracting. After an hour and a quarter had passed in the cold, talking about the weather, Scotland, London, Cambridge, anything to keep silence at bay, the little boy started crying so, flinging off her hat, she decided to play on the man's feelings and, picking up the little coat from the gulley, asked if she could put it on the infant.

When the man hesitated she called to the little boy by name so he turned his head and she walked calmly forward with the coat in her hand, avoiding abrupt movements that would break the comfortable atmosphere that she had built up. Reaching forward as if to put the coat on the infant she grasped him with her right hand as quick as lightning and fell back into the roof, seizing the father with her left at the same time. There is a saying at sea: 'Keep one hand for the boat' meaning, for your own safety, always use one hand to hold onto a nearby fixture while working with the other, particularly in adverse weather. At the instant that she snatched both man and infant neither hand was available for her to save herself and, had the man carried out his stated intention, she would have been dragged over the edge to suffer serious injury at least.

The reactions of the two men on the roof with her were equally speedy and, jumping forward, they secured the man who, with his son, was brought down the stairs at ground level, accompanied by WPC Cleland. A tremendous cheer went up when she appeared outside and she was clapped all the way to the police car, a film of the whole drama being shown that night on television news. Flowers and congratulations swamped the police station next day and she was commended later by the Metropolitan Police Commissioner. After the man's trial on criminal charges the magistrate ordered a contribution be made to her from the Bow Street Police Reward Fund when she appeared on 11 May. She was invested with her George Medal by HM The Queen at Buckingham Palace on 10 November of that year.

Margaret Cleland was born on 20 May 1940 (just after Dunkirk) in Twechar, a mining village just outside Kilsyth, Stirlingshire, one of two daughters of a miner, John Cleland and his wife, Margaret. She went to school at Twechar Junior Secondary School and in 1960 joined the Metropolitan Police on advice from a local police sergeant who had transferred previously from the London force. After initial training at Peel House, Westminster she was posted to north London but at the time of the incident was serving at Gray's Inn Road in Holborn, an officer of medium height, well built with neat, dark hair.

In December 1964 she transferred to the Dunbartonshire Constabulary from where she retired in 1966 and become a post office telephonist in Glasgow. She later joined the civil staff of the police at Bishopbriggs, north Glasgow where she met and married PC Tom Jackson in 1974. Sadly, he died on Christmas Eve 1988 and she now lives on her own in Kilsyth.

The needlework class of thirteen 14/15-year-old girls in St. John's Roman Catholic School, Harefield Road, Dundee, Angus was proceeding peacefully on the afternoon of 1 November 1967 when Mrs Nanette Hanson, the twenty-six-year-old needlework teacher, saw a man standing in the classroom doorway holding a single-barrelled shotgun. At first, the girls treated the whole affair as some sort of joke as he stood there and watched them but, moving in from the top-storey doorway, the man – a nineteen-year-old private soldier of the Gordon Highlanders on leave from his regiment in Germany and a former pupil of the school – ordered the occupants to stand against the wall. He had by now barricaded the two doors with tables and sewing machines and drawn the curtains along the window wall of the room. Threatening the teacher and pupils with the gun he drove them into a small fitting room situated at one end of the main classroom while Mrs Hanson did her best to counter the rising hysteria among the girls. With a small crowd of people gathering outside the classroom door – school authorities, staff and police among them – the soldier fired a shot through the glass door, slightly injuring a woman teacher from the adjoining class who was trying to enter.

Mrs Hanson, summing up the situation coolly, called out to the group outside the door to leave since they could do no good by remaining and shortly afterwards all the other pupils in the school, between 950 and 1,000, were evacuated from the premises. The man continued to threaten the class, assaulting two fourteen-year-olds, pointing the gun at the teacher and pulling the trigger but, fortunately for her at this time, the weapon misfired. It had been mentioned in conversation with him that, some years before, he had known slightly a **Miss Marion Young** who was a pupil nurse at this time in Dundee Royal Infirmary and lived in Dundee so she was asked to come and speak to him. Having been briefed on the dilemma on arrival, she volunteered to go to the needlework room where she was admitted and tried to pacify him, then, after an hour, one of the girls was allowed to leave with a message for the headmaster.

The soldier continued to fire his shotgun at irregular intervals, a total of eight cartridges being fired towards the door. But after requests by the headmaster and others, together with Miss Young's support, all the girls were permitted to leave, none having been hit, although all were in a state of traumatic shock.

At this stage Mrs Hanson had achieved complete moral ascendancy inside the room so, together, the teacher and the nurse tried to persuade the man to refrain from further violence and give to himself up. However, it would appear that he still had an inner compulsion to shoot somebody and, when Mrs Hanson turned to close a window at his request, he shot her in the back as a result of which she died shortly afterwards. Throughout the incident which lasted for two hours, serious problems were created by the people outside trying to deal with the situation although lacking visual contact with the hostages and darkness was setting in early.

Miss Young, a native of Dundee, was born in Clement Park Nursing Home on 21 July 1949, the youngest of two girls and two boys whose father, Ernest Young, was a salesman. She was educated at Rockwell Primary and Secondary schools in the Royal Burgh. Married at St. John's Roman Catholic Church on 7 September 1968 just before taking her finals she did not continue nursing after her marriage, going abroad instead with her husband, Michael Taylor, who was serving in the army. She now lives in Wiltshire with him and their daughter and son.

Mrs Hanson, who came from Ilkley, Yorkshire and was the daughter of a police superintendent, had been married for only six months, her husband being a carpet designer; she had been on the school staff for only two months. She was buried at Ben Rhydigg, Ilkley after a service at St. John's Church in Dundee on Monday 6 November. Her very great gallantry was recognised by the posthumous award of the Albert Medal (Bronze), the award of the gold version having been discontinued in November 1949.

On 16 May 1968 both teacher and nurse were awarded the Sir James Duncan Medal, which had been instituted for members of the public who assist the police by Sir James Duncan, a former MP for Angus. The medals were presented by the Lord Provost of Dundee, Mr Alex Mackenzie, on 12 September 1968. Marion Young had to interrupt her honeymoon to attend the ceremony. The teacher's medal was handed to her mother and father as her husband was then in New Zealand.

The next case with which we are concerned also involved imprisoning people under threat of arms but the motivation this time was money. In the country area of the State of Victoria, Australia, the town of Castlemaine lies some fifty miles north-north-west of Melbourne with the large town of Bendigo twenty-five miles further along the Calder

Highway. Faraday via Castlemaine is a small settlement in the heavily wooded hills at the foot of Mount Alexandra on the highway. Scattered throughout the state of Victoria were 430 small schools with only one teacher each serving the thinly spread population and one of them was at Faraday, a quarter of a mile off the highway. This was a tiny bluestone building, more than a hundred years old, with a corrugated iron roof, and on Friday 6 October 1972 it was occupied by a slim twenty-year-old teacher, **Miss Mary Elizabeth Gibbs**, and six children ranging in age from five to eleven years and coming from three farming families.

They had started the day at 9.30 a.m. Shortly after lunch, while they were playing musical chairs, the door burst open at 1.30 p.m. and two men armed with a sawn-off .22″ rifle rushed in. They told the teacher that they were going to hold her and the children to ransom and that, as it was election year, the ransom demanded from the Government of Victoria would be one million dollars. The teacher and children, Robyn Howarth (11), her sisters Jillian (8) and Denise (5), Lynda Conn (9), Helen Conn (6) and Christine Ellery (10) were herded into the kidnappers' red panel van and driven away. Leaving the ransom note on one of the desks and taking the Calder Highway, they drove by a circuitous route to Lancefield, some forty miles across country, where they concealed the locked van in thick forest.

After some time the children were allowed out to exercise, under threat of instant death should any try to escape. Shortly afterwards they were again locked in and one of the men left the scene. Naturally enough the children were becoming very frightened but Miss Gibbs managed to prevent the situation escalating into one of panic. Meanwhile the parents had arrived at the school to pick up their children. At first, the sight of the teacher's car standing there did not arouse anxiety as it was assumed that she had taken her charges for a walk. The alarm was raised at 3.50 p.m., the ransom note having been found and, eventually, search operations were co-ordinated from the school. At 4.40 p.m., a telephone call was received at the *Melbourne Sun* newspaper, repeating the ransom demand, but the subsequent search operation by the police, St. John's Ambulance Brigade and the general public, together with an aircraft, failed to produce any further clues. Tension in Faraday rose dramatically, particularly in view of the coldness of the night.

Back at Lancefield the kidnap victims were trying desperately to keep warm with the aid of blankets and one pillow thrown into the back of the van but, even huddled together, they suffered after dark from the extreme cold. About 2 a.m. the other man returned bringing some cold chips but these did nothing to relieve the children's hunger as the men settled down in the front seats. Miss Gibb tended the children's needs all night. Just before dawn, the men left in another car to pick up the ransom so, helped by the eldest children, she tried to force the rear door without success.

The van had not been fitted with any windows in the locked area so she decided to attack the panel between this and the front seats. After a period of sustained kicking by the three of them, this was forced, to end their fifteen hours of incarceration. Leading the tired, cold and hungry children away from the van she found a road but was forced to hide each time that the noise of an approaching car was heard. Fearful all the time that the kidnappers would return, teacher and children, after travelling for two miles along a deserted trail through rugged bush, came across two spotlight shooters who took them to Lancefield Police Station. Here they were comforted and their needs attended to, the good news being flashed to Castlemaine and Faraday.

The two men were arrested (one thirty-two years old and the other twenty-one) in February 1973 and charged. On conviction they were sentenced to long terms of imprisonment. In their trial it transpired that they had spent six or seven months planning the crime, considering several schools but had decided on Faraday because it was located some way off the highway. They had dug a trench 14 feet long by 3 feet by 3½ feet which they had covered with corrugated iron and dirt. The victims were to be held in there, chained and padlocked with their mouths taped, and had the plot succeeded, the effects upon the children would have been catastrophically traumatic. The school served an area of twelve square miles but, on the day of the kidnapping, four children on the register had been absent because of illness.

The school remained closed initially for the rest of the year but, sightseers becoming a problem, it was closed permanently and is today used as an adult educational centre. On 23 December 1974 Miss Gibbs was presented with her George Medal in Melbourne by Major General Sir Rohan Delacombe, KBE, CB, DSO, the Governor of the State of Victoria. She left Bendigo in 1974 to teach elsewhere and married Neil Noelkar just over a year after the incident. In 1989 they were living in Swan Hill, northern Victoria (with two sons and two daughters) where he was the Shire Secretary or Chief Executive.

On the south-east coast of New Zealand's South Island lies *Aramoana* (a Maori word meaning 'Pathway of the Sea'), a small remote seaside township on the north-west of the entrance to Otago Harbour. Seventeen miles from Dunedin, the capital of Otago Province, it is positioned on the top of cliffs to the north-west with sand dunes or sandy knolls, dense scrub, tussock grassland, lupins and salt marches to the east and north with a plantation of mature pines at the west end. A further impediment to passage through the area by members of the police in the dark was the presence of mature bramble bushes. Designated a wildlife area, it had only about fifty houses (known locally as 'cribs', no two of which were alike) and a normal population of forty to fifty mostly retired people, very individualistic but strong on community spirit. Life was extremely peaceful. That is, until the evening of Tuesday 13 November 1990, a fine and hot day, when a heavily-armed thirty-three-year-old man embarked on an orgy of killing.

His mother having died in 1985 he lived alone in a house standing on a higher piece of ground in Muri Street. Fascinated by war books and firearms he possessed a gun licence under which he had seven weapons, several of them powerful semi-automatics, and ample supplies of ammunition. Almost blind, wearing strong spectacles without which he could not see clearly beyond half a metre, unstable, embittered, frustrated and unemployed, David Malcolm Grey had been involved in a shouting match with his next-door neighbour, Garry Holden, an automotive engineer by trade who, having contracted ME, had become a natural healer. At about 7.30 p.m. Gray was to shoot this man in a hail of bullets, following this later by killing two of his children in their house and wounding another who escaped. Gray then completed the first stage of his horrific campaign by setting fire to the crib, using a can of petrol.

The call for help was received at 7.51 p.m. at Port Chalmers Police Station, eight miles away, and Sergeant Stewart G. Guthrie, who was in charge, responded although armed only with his offical .38 calibre revolver. A member of the Dunedin armed offenders squad he was a meticulous, highly competent officer, dedicated to the Aramoana community of which he was an active member. Reaching the township he came across, by chance, an off-duty policeman whom he caused to be armed with a borrowed .22 calibre rifle then, together with two other policemen who had just arrived, reconnoitred the area. Although not in radio contact with each other (only the sergeant had a radio link with the police control) they separated to search for the gunman in the fading light.

By this time the gunman, who was armed with two semi-automatic weapons and dressed in commando gear with his face blackened, had embarked on a frenzy of indiscriminate shooting. In it he took the lives of six more adults as they arrived to fight the fire and two more children, wounding another adult and two more children. Around 9 p.m. Sergeant Guthrie located Gray and challenged him in a broken area of tall grass and undergrowth with thick foliage, only to be killed by a burst of fire, the gunman then seizing his police firearm which he soon discarded.

Mrs Eva Helen Dickson, a seventy-two-year-old widow who also lived in a small, neat crib on Muri Street with the eldest of her four sons, Jimmy, was alerted by the sound of shooting and, at about 8.30 p.m., went out to investigate while her son pursued separate inquiries accompanied by his dog. She saw smoke coming from the burning crib and, noticing sixty-one-year-old Christopher Coles, an ex-seaman, walking from Poto Street towards the area from which the sound of shots had come, she tried in vain to dissuade him. While they were talking at the intersection of

Mrs Eva Helen Dickson GM
(photo: Otago Daily Times*).*

Plucky and Muri Streets, the gunman appeared and opened fire and, as they were making for the cover of a nearby telephone box, Mr Coles was wounded by hits in the lower back. The wounded man was powerless to move. Mrs Dickson, because she had two artificial hip joints and restricted movement in her right arm through surgery, was unable to run for cover yet she helped him to the roadside where, mutually unstable, both fell to the ground by the telephone box, she flat on her face. Displaying tremendous courage and resolve in overcoming her disabilities, she dragged herself to her house some fifty metres away from where, having struggled to her feet with the aid of a gatepost, she telephoned urgently for police and ambulance.

This done, she crawled back to Mr Coles and continued to comfort him but, concerned at the apparent lack of response from the emergency services (vehicles were not now being permitted to enter the danger area), she dragged herself back to her home to make further calls. The police, worried about her safety, advised her against returning to Mr Coles but to stay where she was and lock herself in her house, then stay out of sight. After a time two policemen came to the scene in an unarmoured dog van and, with little or no protection from gunfire, skilfully rescued the wounded man after he had lain, face down and appealing for help, for over an hour – but he died an hour later in hospital. Increasingly concerned about the fate of her forty-five-year-old son (in fact, although his dog, covered with blood, had returned shortly after 8.30 p.m., he was now dead, shot several times by Gray), she maintained a lonely tense vigil in her home. She lay on bedding on the kitchen floor between a wall and the refrigerator, her only illumination coming from the burning crib.

Throughout the following night she relayed to her family her commentary on the gunman's movements, performing, alone and voluntarily, the functions of a forward observation officer although every time that she used the telephone she spent up to ten minutes in dragging herself to the instrument. Her third son Alastair and his wife Heather in Port Chalmers were aware of the situation and for three hours telephoned her every quarter of an hour but, realising that the regular sound of the telephone bell was adding to her very considerable danger, the system was changed. Had the gunman suspected her presence in the house there is no doubt that he would have taken determined measures to eliminate her. After 1.15 a.m. it was apparent that Gray was nearby (his footprints were found later on a compost help in the back garden) but she was finally rescued by the police at 4.30 p.m. to be reunited with her family at Port Chalmers Fire Station. It was here that she was given the tragic news that Jimmy was already dead and the last faint flickering hope was extinguished.

All these activities took place in an area of only 150 metres radius, dominated for 22½ hours in both darkness and daylight by the threat from the deranged gunman. Eventually, after two constables, in the face of heavy fire, had attempted to lob tear gas grenades into the crib in which he was hiding, the gunman burst into the open offering defiance and fire from the hip and was killed. His final death toll was one policeman, eight civilian adults and four children with another two children wounded, but the nine-year-old ran to obtain help and warn neighbours in spite of having already lost her father and elder sister. In addition to Mrs Dickson's George Medal, one posthumous George Cross (Sergeant Guthrie), one posthumous Queen's Gallantry Medal, four Queen's Gallantry Medals and five Queen's Commendations for Brave Conduct (one to the wounded girl Chiquita Holden) were awarded.

Mrs Dickson received her medal from the hands of the Governor General of New Zealand, Dame Catherine Tizard, GCMG, DBE at the Dunedin Civic Centre, on 23 October 1992 at which ceremony the other awards were presented to the winners or their next of kin. She was the first New Zealand woman to be awarded the medal and first woman anywhere for almost nineteen years.

Born in Maori Hill, Dunedin on 28 September 1919 Eva Helen was one of four children of James Craighead, a health inspector, and his wife Eva Holmes Craighead. She was educated at Maori Hill Primary School, Dunedin North Intermediate School and King Edward Technical School, then worked as a nurse. On 16 December 1942 she married Neil Alexander Rogerson Dickson, a die-caster, at Maori Hill Presbyterian Church but was widowed in 1976.

The Dickson family had been connected with the Muri Street crib since 1939 but, after the incident, her first reaction was that she wished to sever all connections with it. Her son Jimmy, a caring gentle man, had lived there and had been fully supportive although he worked as the bindery manager in the Dunedin Public Library where he is now commemorated by a memorial plaque. He used to drive her to Port Chalmers and Dunedin when required and helped around the house, even hanging out the washing because of her problems. She decided to sell the crib but changed her mind when her grandson said that if she did he would never speak to her again. Her interests, aside from her family of course, are now reading and bowls.

Chapter 8

Saving Life in other Circumstances

ALL activities considered to be suitable for the award of the George Medal involve saving life, directly or indirectly, at the risk of the rescuer's own. Those concerned with air-raids, resistance/underground work or the fight against crime have been dealt with in the preceding chapers so this final chapter deals with life-saving attempts in other situations, both war and peace. Reactions to danger differed in each according to the variety of pressures being exerted by the special circumstances. Additionally, each individual can be said to have approached the problem facing him or her from the viewpoint of personal ability, bringing to bear judgement and making decisions in the light of personality, training and experience.

From the start of the war an essential part of the Air Raid Precautions Organisation (ARP – later to be re-named 'Civil Defence') was the provision of a large number of ambulances, crewed on either a part-time or a full-time basis. This was not to say, however, that they were limited to call-out solely under air-raid conditions and, on the morning of Monday 8 July 1940 (before the medal was conceived) there was no air-raid warning in force at Aldeburgh, a town on the Suffolk coast between Southwold and Ipswich. With the British and Allied forces pushed out of France and Belgium the United Kingdom was now in a ferment of setting up anti-invasion measures, a vital element of which was the laying of defensive minefields on all vulnerable beaches, marshes and other remote coastal areas, a measure made even more urgent by the shortage of available military manpower for other forms of defence.

Mrs Dorothy Clarke GM; Mrs Bessie Jane Hepburn GM (photo: Imperial War Museum).

Millions of mines, many of them powerful and sensitive weapons containing 25 pounds of high explosive, had been laid around the coasts, their presence and the extent of the fields of death often indicated only by a few strands of barbed wire. The beaches north and south of Aldeburgh comprise mainly shingle and large pebbles, a difficult medium in which to lay and mark minefields the extent of which were so ill-defined. For reasons no longer apparent, although it must be said that at this stage of the war few troops had had any experience of mines or their potential lethality, two soldiers strayed into a heavily mined area on Thorpeness beach at the mouth of the Hundred River, accidentally setting off a mine.

The resulting explosion was reported to the ARP Services so the Aldeburgh ambulance, crewed by **Mrs Dorothy Clarke** as driver with **Mrs Bessie Jane Knight-Hepburn** (gazetted only as 'Hepburn') as her attendant, was ordered to the scene. Arriving on the beach after a two mile journey, they found one of the casualties already dead and the other gravely injured. In spite of a firm warning from experts on the scene that such a course would be extremely dangerous, no doctor being present, these two ladies, advancing into middle age in comfortable circumstances, took a stretcher to the injured man and rendered first aid before carrying him back to the ambulance. In fact, when warned of the danger, Mrs Knight-Hepburn's reply was, 'It is our job to look after the wounded, wherever they may be.' Unfortunately, the wounded man died later after admission to Aldeburgh Hospital.

Mrs Knight-Hepburn, married to an Aldeburgh chemist, was forty-two years old at the time and, in June 1946, took part in the London Victory March as the representative of the East Anglia St. John's Ambulance. When she died in 1974 she had been a widow for some years, living at and running a dog kennels business in Wickham Skeith, near Eye, Suffolk. Mrs Clarke, who was thirty-eight years old when she entered the minefield, was born in Leamington Spa, Warwickshire. After her marriage to Mr Geoffrey Clarke, a government official in Burma, they had returned to England and, settling in Aldeburgh, were to run an apple orchard after the war. Following her husband's death she moved to Lavenham, Suffolk where she died in 1981.

The names of both women appeared in the first George Medal *London Gazette Supplement* and they were invested by HM The King at Buckingham Palace on 27 May 1941 wearing their ARP uniforms. Their medals are now displayed at the Moot Hall in Aldeburgh as a tribute to two brave women who, without regard for their own safety, tried to save the lives of others.

Basic aircrew training, uninterrupted by enemy action, was becoming increasingly difficult in the United Kingdom in the second year of the war. So, as the production of replacement aircrew, together with the increased numbers demanded by a growing Air Force, was vital to the

Mrs Frances Walsh GM
(photo: Mrs Olive Jesluch).

prosecution of the war effort, the Empire Flying Training Scheme (later the Commonwealth Air Training Plan) was introduced. In this, candidates were posted to initial training schools scattered throughout the Empire (as it was known) and the United States of America before being assigned to more advanced training prior to posting to operational flying duties. Opportunity was also taken to absorb local candidates. One such installation was No. 2 Wireless School at Calgary, Alberta in Canada from where Leading Aircraftman K.M. Gravell, RCAF, aged eighteen was flying as a Wireless Operator/Air Gunner under training in a two seater Tiger Moth biplane on Monday 10 November 1941.

During this flight, at 11 a.m., the aircraft crashed into the schoolyard of Big Springs School, seven miles north of the Banff Highway and twenty-five miles north-west of Calgary. After hitting the ground just inside the schoolyard and narrowly missing a school building it struck the ground again, breaking through a fence and, bursting into flames, came to a stop twenty-five yards away at the bottom of a deep gulley. The trainee WOp/AG sustained serious burns and injuries which included the loss of an eye but, having extricated himself from the wreckage, in spite of intense shock, his only thought was to rescue his pilot instructor, Flying Officer James Robinson (44), not knowing whether this other victim was alive or dead. The mass of flames engulfed the intending rescuer, causing severe burns all over his body and forcing him to retire just before **Mrs Frances Walsh** (wrongly spelt 'Francis' in *London Gazette Supplement*), the thirty-one-year-old school teacher at the school, arrived to find him in the blazing wreckage again still engaged in his desperate rescue effort.

Faced by totally strange circumstances involving the ever-present danger of petrol explosions, this pretty teacher nevertheless reacted immediately without thought of personal safety, running into the holocaust and dragging out the airman. Throwing him to the ground, she rolled him over in the dust to extinguish the flames on his clothing. This done, helped by her pupils, she carried him to her house where she rendered first aid and caused medical asistance to be summoned by telephone. In doing all this she was burned about her face and hair as well as sustaining shock but made no comment on her own condition until, the medical team having arrived in two aircraft and road ambulances, the LAC had been treated. He was evacuated by ambulance to the Colonel Belcher Hospital in Calgary where he died in the afternoon.

Mrs Walsh was invested with her medal by the Governor General of Canada, Major General The Earl of Athlone, KG, PC, GCB, GCMG,GCVO, DSO, FRS, ADC at Ottawa on 3 December 1942, the RCAF having flown her and her parents there for the ceremony.

The pilot instructor had been killed in the crash and a posthumous George Cross was awarded to LAC Gravell (LG 11 June 1942).

Frank Hamlin went to Canada from Wiltshire, England and married Annie Deller who came from Brockville, Ontario. They had three daughters and a son, the eldest daughter, Frances, being born in Sandstone, Alberta (a small town which no longer exists), south of Calgary on 21 October 1910. Frances Hamlin studied at Eagle School and Central High School before getting her teaching certificate at Normal School, all in the Calgary area. In 1930 she started teaching in a small country school at Carrot Creek nearly a hundred miles west of Edmonton on the Yellowhead Highway where she met and married Ken Walsh and, in 1937, gave birth to a son (who, having joined the RCAF, was by a bizarre and tragic coincidence killed in a training flight accident in 1955).

Later, in 1937, she started teaching at Big Springs School, another small school dealing with children up to thirteen years old, where the accident occurred in November 1942. Little over 5′4″, of medium build, she had brown hair and blue eyes and was very attractive. After a period of recuperation she went to teach at a large school in Bowness, just west of Calgary, working at a munitions plant in Pickering, Ontario in her summer holidays. In 1947 she moved west to Vancouver Island to work for Victoria Water District before going to live in Vancouver City in 1949 to work with an export company, continuing with them until her early death from the effects of cancer in October 1961, greatly mourned. She is buried in Powell River, BC on the Strait of Georgia.

The scene of the next award-winning action in this category could not be much farther away from Calgary and it is difficult to imagine surroundings and activities more different in every aspect. Across the Pacific Ocean Australian forces were heavily engaged on operations in New Guinea guarding the left flank of the American fight-back from unrelieved disasters in the south-western Pacific and countering the Japanese thrust towards Australia. Supported by naval and air forces their land battles were fought with utmost ferocity in the most atrocious conditions – mountainous, steaming jungle terrain honeycombed with Japanese bunkers and tunnels, in tropical rain and constantly sweat-soaked clothing, staggering heat allied to disease and physical degeneration and, more often than not, opposed by a cunning, unrelenting unseen enemy.

In that pre-helicopter era the standard form of battle casualty evacuation was using makeshift stretchers carried along jungle paths, a difficult operation made more wearying for their comrades by having to concentrate on retaining their own footing in slimy treacherous mud. These comrades were often exhausted to the point of indifference – almost but not quite because these were loyal, stubborn, individualistic Aussies helping a 'mate', knowing that when the casualty reached organised medical aid, he would be evacuated to Australia where his chances of survival and recovery would be improved out of all recognition.

An essential link in that journey was provided by ships equipped and staffed as floating hospitals, one of which was the 3,222-ton Australian Hospital Ship *Centaur* (Ocean Steam Ship Co Ltd) on charter to the Admiralty and taken into use on 1 March 1943. On her second voyage to New Guinea to embark casualties, brightly lit and painted in the distinctive red crosses and green stripe livery demanded by the Geneva Convention, she was struck at 4 a.m. on 14 May 1943 when a Japanese submarine fired two torpedoes which penetrated the port side fuel tank, abaft No. 2 Hatch opening. The oil caught fire immediately and three minutes later the ship sank at 27°17′ South, 154°05′ East, forty miles east-south-east of Brisbane, Queensland. With 2/12 Field Ambulance, RAAMC on board, normal duties, interrupted by four practice boat drills, had occupied the day and the evening had passed quietly, everybody not on duty retiring by 10 p.m.

After the torpedoes struck, **Lieut. Ellen Savage**, Australian Army Nursing Service (AANS) hurried on deck wearing only her lifebelt over her pyjamas but, while making for her lifeboat station, was told by the commanding officer to jump overboard rather than go back for her greatcoat. She did this in company with others but, as the ship sank, she was dragged down in the terrible, suction-induced whirlpool until entirely breathless before she started to rise towards the surface. The intense vice-like pressure of water left her with fractured ribs, nose and palate, perforated ear drums and multiple bruising but she reached the surface in spite of having been entangled in ropes and struck by sinking debris – the only one of the twelve AANS nurses to survive.

A well-built, handsome woman with a striking personality she was of above average height, her fairish hair conspicuous in the sea. The middle of three daughters of an immigrant tailer and his Australian wife, Ellen Savage was born in Quirindi, northern New South Wales, 380 miles north of Sydney, on 17 October 1912 and educated at the convent school in Quirindi run by the Sisters of St. Joseph. She qualified as a nurse at the Royal Newcastle Hospital, did her midwifery training at Crown Street Hospital, Sydney and then her baby care training at the Tresillian Centre after which she worked at baby health care centres in New South Wales until she joined the AANS on 30 October 1941 as Staff Nurse, being promoted Sister Group 1 on 22 March 1943. Up to that time, despite having officer status, members of the AANS were not commissioned officers although, when on active service, they became subject to military law and were on the same footing as accredited correspondents and representatives of philanthropic bodies. In March 1943, under changed regulations, they became commissioned officers and on 23 March she was appointed lieutenant and seconded to the Australian Imperial Forces in which rank she was posted to *Centaur*.

A strong swimmer, she joined an orderly who was swimming to a piece of wreckage, the roof of one of the deckhouses, and, balancing upon it, they floated about until 8 a.m. with other people swimming around and scrambling upon whatever debris was available. None of the lifeboats had been launched but several life rafts had floated clear and, at this time, they came near one that was already crowded but those on board decided, unselfishly, to make room for Miss Savage and the orderly. A brave West Australian man swam across with the end of a piece of rope in his mouth then pulled the raft to them so that they were able to step from their precarious perch. It was then that, as they floated away from the oily surface created by the *Centaur's* leaking tanks, they saw their first sharks.

During the day they tied up with other rafts and on them more than thirty survivors floated around surrounded by hoards of both tiger and nurse sharks which frequently attacked and shook their rafts. One or two badly burned men died that night, another eleven nurses and 257 crew and medical staff having been lost in the attack. The survivors were to drift for thirty-four hours during which they sighted four ships and several aircraft but they themselves were not seen. A submarine surfaced during the night and moods of elation gave way to despondency but, during the whole time Miss Savage attended the wounded and those suffering from burns, maintaining the morale of all of her companions by example and personality until they were sighted finally by an RAAF aircraft which directed the American destroyer USS *Mugford* to them. Sixty-four survivors were picked up.

After survivors' leave following the rescue Miss Savage was posted to No. 113 (Concord) Military Hospital in Sydney from where she was placed on the Reserve of Officers on 9 March 1946. She did not attend an investiture or presentation, her medal being sent to her from Canberra, ACT on 26 August 1947.

After she left the army she returned to baby health care centres and in 1947 was awarded a Red Cross Scholarship which took her on the first Florence Nightingale Scholarship to a post-graduate course on administration at the Royal College of Nursing in London. After a period back at her old training school, Royal Newcastle Hospital, she was appointed Matron of Rankin Park Hospital, a subsidiary of the Royal Newcastle. Ill health forced her to retire in 1967 when she had a stroke from which she made a fairly good recovery. Sadly, she died attending what to her was the event of the year, the reunion of survivors of the *Centaur* after the Anzac Day Parade on 25 April 1985 in Sydney. As she was leaving she collapsed and died on the steps of Sydney Hospital, much mourned, and is buried in Northern Suburbs Cemetery, Sydney, her grave marked by a War Graves Commission headstone.

With the end of the Second World War in 1945 vast stocks of ammunition and explosives remained unused, a significant quantity of which had been in the hands of user units where it had been expected that these materials would have been expended against the enemy. In the post-war years a vast programme of back-loading was in train intended either to return these items to stock or to prepare them for safe disposal. Each of these alternatives required every unsealed item to be examined to establish its degree of safety or, if necessary, to make it safe. Massive increases in the storage demand as the war had progressed, particularly after the Dunkirk evacuation, meant that the permanent storage became, as far as the army was concerned, totally inadequate, so temporary 'field storage' depots (known as Ammunition Supply Depots) using small corrugated iron shelters sprang up all over the United Kingdom.

In the depot – 32 ASD – at Saxelbye, Leicestershire, three miles west of Melton Mowbray, work was in progress on Wednesday 14 January 1948, inspecting and repacking anti-tank mine fuses, a particularly sensitive store especially if it had at some time been laid in the ground and subsequently recovered. The inspection/repair area consisted of four rows of nissen huts beside a road leading to Six Hills Road in an area known as Saxelbye Pastures, half a mile from the village. Conditions in the hut where the work was taking place were primitive, earth floor and no heating in spite of the bitter cold. This work force was a mixed team of RAOC and RPC soldiers under Sergeant (A/S Sgt) Ken Nash, RAOC, an ammunition examiner. Each fuse contained a comparatively large explosive charge. The fuses were packed in metal cylinders in a wooden crate, each holding about four pounds of high explosive, and there were many crates in the hut.

During the morning a serious explosion occurred killing two private soldiers of the RPC and severely injuring eight others, one of whom died in hospital later. There was no telephone in the working area and the nearest private one was found to be out of action so another, farther away, had to be used to summon help. Where a military unit was not big enough to warrant a medical officer of its own there was a procedure involving a system of rounds operated from major units in the locality. At the time, Lieutenant J. McLenachan, RAMC from the Royal Leicestershire Regiment barracks was conducting a sick parade in the nearby accommodation camp accompanied by **Lance-Corporal Margaret Emma Richards**, Auxiliary Territorial Service (ATS), a medical orderly from Central Ordnance Depot, Old Dalby, three miles to the west. Hurrying to the scene of the explosion, they found the working area with casualities and loose unexploded fuses in a setting of violent, dangerous confusion and disarray.

Curved corrugated iron sheets from the skin of the nissen hut had been torn off, leaving a long jagged hole in its roof, broken wood and metal fragments being scattered on the approach path and floor. Although warned very seriously of the extreme danger of further explosions they went into the wrecked hut, picking their way through other apparently unexploded fuses which had been projected outside the hut, and started to attend the casualties. Two badly mutilated corpses were lying on the floor. Despite the unpleasant sickening sight and the dangerous debris, L.Cpl. Richards displayed great coolness in helping the medical officer in his ministrations to the gravely injured soldiers. Despite being warned again by S.Sgt. Nash, in no uncertain terms, of

Pte. Margaret E. Richards GM
(photo: Mrs M. E. Crooks).

the danger she continued to help the MO in attending the injured men who had been taken to another hut – these were in a panicky state since some of them were unable to see or breathe properly.

She set out to calm them, talking cheerfully and jollying them along, showing an excellent grasp of her duties, helping the MO to arrest haemorrhage, improvise splinting and expose and treat their wounds. Throughout the whole time that she spent in the area she was an inspiration to the men around her, her cheerfulness and courage under dangerous and unpleasant conditions being exemplary while her efficiency was outstanding in preparing the injured men for transport to Leicester Royal Infirmary. Shirking no aspect of her disagreeable task she was instrumental, in all probability, in preventing further loss of life in the presence of great danger. Lt. McLenachan and S.Sgt. Nash were each awarded the George Medal as well, their investitures, perforce, taking place on different dates. Margaret Richards, however, was invested with her medal by HM The King at Buckingham Palace on 2 November 1949, accompanied by one of her sisters.

Born at Hanbury near Burton-on-Trent, Staffordshire on 11 July 1923, one of four daughters of Thomas Richards, a farm worker, and his wife Daisy (née Cook), she went to school in Hoar Cross, Newborough and then in Draycott, both Staffordshire, and started work as an under-housemaid at Doveridge in Derbyshire where she fell victim to scarlet fever. She was admitted to Etwall Isolation Hospital, between Burton-on-Trent and Derby, where, after recovering, she started work, aged fifteen, but left suffering from malnutrition. This was followed by a period as a children's nanny on a farm in Fole, near Uttoxeter, which put her back on her feet again. On 13 March 1942 she joined the ATS, reporting to Pontefract, West Riding, Yorkshire where, after training, she joined the camp staff before being posted to a unit in Wimbledon.

While there she attended a medical course at Bovington, Dorset but was demobilised in April 1946, taking up private work looking after an invalid lady in Abbot's Bromley where her mother lived in Bagot Street. However, missing service life, she re-enlisted in February 1947, working as a medical orderly at Leamington Spa and Coventry before being posted to Old Dalby. At the time of the explosion she was a slim, smart twenty-five-year-old wearing the ribbons of the Defence and War Medals and, before her award had been gazetted, she was posted to 27 Vehicle Reserve Depot, RAOC on Bardney airfield just outside Lincoln from where she went to a large unit at Harwich, Essex.

At that time her interests were children and animals and her hobbies were riding, cricket, cycling and walking. Demobilised again on 15 May 1949 she worked as a night nurse at Rugeley District Hospital then, on 7 February 1953, married Francis Douglas Crooks, a lorry driver and small-holder, at Hanbury Parish Church. They lived in Derby and, between 1953 and 1961, had three daughters and a son but, her husband having died in January 1962, she moved from Derby in March 1964. No stranger to hardship or straitened circumstances she is living, with her youngest daughter, in Abbot's Bromley, her interests now her grandchildren, gardening and animals.

At 3.55 a.m. on Easter Sunday, 18 April 1954 **Miss Freda Holland**, Night Sister, was on duty with a Sister Thomas in Dellwood Maternity Home, Reading, Berkshire. Born at Pulborough, Sussex in January 1913, her father a farmer, Miss Holland was to have two brothers and to be educated at Ramsgate Grammar School, Kent. She trained at Manchester Royal Infirmary, qualifying in general nursing in May 1943, following this by training in midwifery in which she qualified in March 1945 at East End Maternity Hospital, London, a temporary hospital set up as a result of the war. Her training continued at Polly Farm, Sulhampstead, near Reading, another emergency maternity unit. After this she went to work in Worthing Maternity Hospital, Sussex before taking the appointment at Reading.

Paying a routine visit to the first floor nursery where fifteen babies were accommodated, she opened the door to be met with dense smoke so, while her companion went to telephone for help, she went into the nursery. Ignoring the danger to herself she fought her way in turn to each baby, picking it up and passing it to Sister Thomas who, having now returned, took it to safety. This rescue activity involved Sister Holland in frequent entry through the dense smoke into the nursery and, once inside, she had to avoid those parts of the floor which were now burning. In doing this she sustained burns to her arms, legs and face. Having brought out all fifteen babies, she was led away from the nursery by firemen but resisted them, still insisting on attending to her charges after they had been taken downstairs.

Still protesting, she eventually collapsed and it was necessary for her to be ordered to another hospital where she underwent immediate skin-grafting operations which left her badly scarred about the arms and face, her sight having been affected as well. Tragically, owing to the effects of smoke, only two babies survived but, because of her illness, this information was withheld from her until some time later. It was necessary for her investiture to be delayed but on 2 November 1954 she received her medal from Her Majesty The Queen at Buckingham Palace.

She took some time to recover from the effects of the fire, returning to work on 1 October, and carried on general nursing until 1958 when, having already trained to be a Queen's District Nurse, she took up that work, remaining in it until she retired in January 1973. Her father having died in 1942 she was living with her mother at the time of the fire then, when her mother died in 1955, she moved to another address in Reading where she now lives.

A police officer, Assistant Inspector J.W. Maxwell of the Northern Rhodesia Police, was swimming in the Kafue River at Mr W. Cox's farm by the Solwezi Road, eighteen miles west-south-west of Chingola, Northern Rhodesia (now Zambia) on 10 December 1961. Swimming with him were three boys, aged seven, nine and twelve. When a large crocodile was seen between them and the river bank he shouted a warning to the boys and he directed them to a rock projecting from the river. The nine-year-old managed to scramble to safety with his help but, owing to the rock's slipperiness and their being petrified with fear, the other two were unable to reach safety. When the crocodile was seen to be advancing toward them Mr Maxwell jumped between it and the two children, voluntarily placing himself in a position of extreme danger.

Disregarding this, he succeeded in helping both boys onto the rock but, while dealing with the second one, the inspector was seized by the reptile. He reacted by beating it on the snout and in the eye, forcing it to release him but he was seized again before he could reach the rock and dragged into deep water. Knowing that this action was the preliminary to the crocodile drowning him so that it could return later to devour him at leisure he summoned up hidden reserves of strength and opened the attacker's jaws, releasing his leg. He then gouged out its eye using his fingers and forced it to let go altogether although, by now, his left foot was almost severed and his right arm badly mauled. Leaving a dangerous trail of blood he managed to swim to the rock onto which he was able to climb then, helped by the children, succeeded in tearing up a towel which he applied to his leg as a tourniquet.

Alerted by the children's cries for help during the rescue, **Mrs Belini Maloni**, a nineteen-year-old African woman who was a children's nurse at Ballybush Farm nearby, ran to the scene. Unable to swim and ignoring the probability that other crocodiles would be attracted by the blinded attacker now thrashing violently about in the water, she entered the river. Wading across to the rock she helped the inspector onto her back them, although terrified, crawled through the water to the bank on her hands and knees. Mother of two children herself her suppression of her natural terror in the presence of these horrifying reptiles in carrying out this action made it possible for the inspector to be given rapid medical attention essential to his survival. Inspector Maxwell was also awarded the George Medal and Mrs Maloni was invested with hers by the Governor of Northern Rhodesia, Sir Evelyn Hone, KCMG, CVO, OBE at Kitwe on 8 September 1962.

No trace could be found of her at the time of writing.

A few days before Christmas 1965 a man was admitted to the Middlesex Hospital, a large building in Marylebone standing at the junction of Mortimer and Cleveland Streets in London's West End. While going through the routine admission procedure a pen-knife was found among his personal effects but he refused to surrender it. On Christmas Eve, just after dark, he was seen to leave the ward and make for the landing of an internal fire escape. A nurse who was following him saw him mount one flight of stairs then, before she could stop him, open a window and climb out onto a narrow ledge which ran across the face of the building level with the fifth floor saying that he was going to commit suicide by throwing himself off. When **Miss Fiona Janet Maud Chard**, the ward sister, heard what had happened she rushed to another window in the direction that he was taking and climbed out onto the ledge so that she could intercept him.

After negotiating a particularly dangerous point at a right-angled corner of the building she came face to face with him and began attempts to dissuade him from jumping off. He was a tall well-built man but, nevertheless, she, a slim woman, tried to restrain him, holding onto him although he thrusted her away. He continued to resist on the ledge which was only twenty inches wide with a sheer drop to the courtyard a hundred feet below. The wall lacked any projection or handhold and it was dark and drizzling with rain at the time but Miss Chard, although aware of his mental state and the fact that he possessed a knife, continued to reason with him despite the appalling danger. Not long after she had become involved in the perilous situation Mr M.G. Johnson, a surgical registrar, came into the ward. Learning of the circumstances, he climbed onto the ledge, having decided to approach from the other side of the patient.

Working together, nurse and surgeon acted in concert to prevent the patient from jumping, pleading with him and physically restraining him while running immense risks since, on that narrow, slippery ledge, they could not fail to be dragged down with him were he to jump or fall. After half an hour of reasoning he was induced to climb back through the window and, having been pacified, was transferred to a mental hospital later that evening. Both participants having been awarded the George Medal, they were invested with their medals by HM The Queen at Buckingham Palace on 12 July 1966.

Sister Chard was born in Kampala, the capital of Uganda, where her father was the Government Printer of that East African country from 1950. She went to school in Kenya before being trained at the Middlesex Hospital where she qualified in 1960. In the spring of 1967 she left the Middlesex to marry her partner in the dramatic struggle on the ledge, Mr Johnson – the only instance of husband and wife each having been awarded the George Medal for the same incident. He was appointed to the post of Consultant Surgeon in West Dorset in 1967 and they now live in Frampton, near Dorchester, with their son and daughter.

Appendix A

The George Medal
Royal Warrant

GEORGE R.I.

GEORGE THE SIXTH, by the Grace of God, of Great Britain, Ireland and the British Dominions beyond the Sea, King, Defender of the Faith, Emperor of India, to all whom these Presents shall come,

GREETING!

WHEREAS We have taken into Our Royal consideration the many acts of great bravery performed both by male and by female persons especially during the present war:

And whereas We are desiring of honouring those who perform such deeds:

We do by these Presents for Us, Our Heirs and Successors institute and create a new Medal.

First: It is ordained that the Medal shall be designated and styled 'The George Medal'.

Secondly: It is ordained that the medal shall be circular in form and in silver, that it shall bear on the obverse the Crowned Effigy of the Sovereign and on the reverse a representation of St. George slaying the Dragon on the coast of England, the design circumscribed by the words 'The George Medal'.

Thirdly: It is ordained that the persons eligible for the medal shall be –

(1) Our faithful subjects and persons under Our protection in civil life, male and female, of Our United Kingdom of Great Britain and Northern Ireland, India, Burma, Our Colonies and of Territories under Our Suzerainty, Protection and Jurisdiction.

(2) Persons of any rank in the Naval, Military or Air Forces of Our United Kingdom of Great Britain and Northern Ireland, of India, of Burma, of Our Colonies, and of Territories under Our Suzerainty, Protection or Jurisdiction, including the Home Guard and members of the Indian States' Forces and in Burma members of the Burma Frontier Force and Military Police, and including also the Military Nursing Services and the Women's Auxiliary Services.

(3) Our faithful subjects and persons under Our protection in civil life, male and female, within, and members of the Naval, Military and Air Forces belonging to, any Member country of the Commonwealth, other than Our United Kingdom, the Government whereof has signified its desire that the Medal should be awarded under the provisions of this Warrant, and any Territory being administered by Us in such Government.

The Medal is intended primarily for civilians and award in Our military service is to be confined to actions for which purely military honours are not normally granted.

Fourthly: It is ordained that awards shall be made on a recommendation to Us, for civilians by Our Prime Minister and the First Lord of the Treasury, and for Officers and members of Our Naval, Military or Air Forces as described in the previous clause of this Warrant, only on a recommendation by Our First Lord of the Admiralty, Our Secretary of State for War or Our Secretary of State for Air, as the case may be.

Fifthly: It is ordained that the Medal shall be awarded only for acts of great bravery.

Sixthly: It is ordained that foreign persons shall be eligible for the award of the Medal and that awards to such persons not included in the Third Clause of this Our Warrant shall be made only on a recommendation to Us for civilians by Our Secretary of State for Foreign Affairs and for Officers and members of foreign military Forces by Our First Lord of the Admiralty, Our Secretary of State for War or Our Secretary of State for Air as the case may be.

Seventhly: It is ordained that the Medal shall be worn by recipients on the left breast suspended from a ribbon one-and-a-quarter inches in width, of red, with five equidistant narrow vertical stripes of blue, and that it shall be worn immediately after the King's Police and Fire Services Medal for gallantry.

Provided that when the Medal is worn by a woman, it may be worn on the left shoulder, suspended from a ribbon of the same width and colour fashioned into a bow.

Eighthly: It is ordained that the award of the Medal shall entitle the recipient, on all occasions when the use of such letters is customary to have placed after his or her names the letters 'G.M.'

Ninthly: It is ordained that an action which is worthy of recognition by the award of the Medal, but is performed by one upon whom the Medal has been conferred, may be recorded by the award of a Bar to be attached to the ribbon by which the Medal is suspended, that for each additional award an additional Bar shall be added and that for each Bar awarded a silver rosette shall be added to the ribbon when worn alone.

Tenthly: It is ordained that the names of all those upon whom We may be pleased to confer or present the Medal, or a Bar to the Medal, shall be published in the London Gazette, and that a Register of such names shall be kept in the Central Chancery of the Orders of Knighthood.

Eleventhly: It is ordained that reproductions of the Medal, known as a Miniature Medal, which may be worn on certain occasions by those to whom the Medal is awarded shall be half the size of the George Medal.

Twelfthly: It is ordained that it shall be competent for Us, Our Heirs and Successors by an Order under Our Sign Manual and on a recommendation to that effect by or through Our Prime Minister and First Lord of the Treasury, Our First Lord of the Admiralty, Our Secretary of State for War or Our Secretary of State for Air, as the case may be, to cancel or annul the award to any person of the George Medal and that thereupon the name of such person in the Register shall be erased: provided that it shall be competent for Us, Our Heirs and Successors to restore the Medal so forfeited when such recommendation has been withdrawn.

Lastly: We reserve to Ourself, Our Heirs and Successors, full power of annulling, altering, abrogating, augmenting, interpreting or dispensing with these rules and ordinances, or any part thereof, by a notification under Our Sign Manual.

Given at Our Court of St James's, the twenty-fourth of September, one thousand nine hundred and forty, in the fourth year of Our Reign.

By His Majesty's Command,

Winston S. Churchill

(for amendments see page 3)

Appendix B

Alphabetical List of Women Awarded the George Medal

Name and Occupation	Place and Date	Reference	*London Gazette* date and page
ANDERSON, *Lieut.* (Staff Nurse) Margaret. VX 63845. *Australian Army Nursing Service.*	Durien Strait, Dutch East Indies. *12 February 1942*	Chap. 4	22 Sep 42 *p. 4123*
ANDERSON, *Miss* Vera. S.R.N. Nurse. *Boots Pure Drug Co., Ltd.*	Nottingham. *8/9 May 1941*	Chap. 3	18 Jul 41 *p. 4106*
APOSTOLIDES, *Miss* Sylvia. Doctor's daughter.	Athens and area, Greece. *September 1943 to 23 September 1944*	Chap. 6	20 Nov 48*
BATEMAN, *Dr.* Laura. *M.B., Ch.B.* Medical Officer. *Brook Hospital.*	Shooter's Hill, London. *29 January 1941*	Chap. 1	13 Jun 41 *p. 3364*
BEARDSHALL, *Mrs.* May. Portress. *Coventry and Warwickshire Hospital.*	Coventry, Warwickshire. *8/9 April 1941*	Chap. 3	8 May 41 *p. 4546*
BICK, *Miss* Charity. Despatch Rider. *A.R.P. Service.*	West Bromwich, Warwickshire. *19 November 1940*	Chap. 3	14 Feb 41 *p. 870*
BILLIG, *Dr.* Hannah. *M.B., B.S.* Medical Practitioner.	Stepney, London. *8 March 1941*	Chap. 1	27 Jun 41 *p. 3646*

BOULTON, *Mrs.* Marian, Edith. *S.R.N.*, *S.C.M.*, *L.R.A.M.* Matron. *Sir Robert Geffrey's Homes.*	Mottingham, London. *10 September 1940*	Chap. 1	25 Apr 41 *p. 2336*
BROWN, *Miss* Margaret. Works Nurse. *Alfred Herbert Ltd.*	Coventry, Warwickshire. *10/11 April 1941*	Chap. 3	7 Jul 41 *p. 3894*
BURTON, *Miss* Joyce Elizabeth. *S.R.N.*, *S.C.M.* Matron. *Coventry and Warwickshire Hospital.*	Coventry, Warwickshire. *8/9 April 1941*	Chap. 3	7 Jul 41 *p. 3894*
BUSH, *Miss* Ethel Violet. Woman Police Sergeant. *Metropolitan Police.*	Croydon, Surrey. *23 April 1955*	Chap. 7	14 Jun 55 *p. 3450*
CHARD, *Miss* Fiona Janet Maud. Ward Sister. *Middlesex Hospital.*	West End, London. *24 December 1965*	Chap. 8	5 Apr 66 *p. 3933*
CLARKE, *Mrs.* Dorothy. Driver. *Ambulance Service.*	Aldeburgh, Suffolk. *8 July 1940*	Chap. 8	30 Sep 40 *p. 5768*
CLELAND, *Miss* Margaret Shaw. Woman Police Constable. *Metropolitan Police.*	Bloomsbury, London. *4 March 1964*	Chap. 7	18 Aug 64 *p. 7077*
COLLINS, *Mrs.* Edith Gladys. Nursing Sister.	Laucula Bay, Suva, Fiji. *9/10 May 1958*	Chap. 7	2 Dec 58 *p. 7361*
DICKSON, *Mrs.* Eva Helen. Housewife	Aramoana, Dunedin, South Island, New Zealand. *13/14 November 1990*	Chap. 7	18 Feb 92† *p.2784*
DUMONT, *Mlle.* Aline, Lily. Member. *'Comet' Escape Line.*	Belgium, France and Spain. *September 1942 to 22 June 1944*	Chap. 5	8 Aug 45*
EDE, *Miss* Rose. Farmer's daughter.	Wadhurst, Sussex. *30 September 1940*	Chap. 2	13 Dec 40 *p. 7018*
FITZGERALD, *Mrs.* Mary. Driver. *First Aid Unit.*	Plymouth, Devon. *29 April 1941*	Chap. 2	8 Aug 41 *p. 4546*
FLEMING, *Miss* Mary. Staff Nurse. *Grove Park Hospital.*	Grove Park, London. *19 November 1940*	Chap. 1	9 May 41 *p. 2639*

FOLMER, *Miss* Johanna Maria. Student. Member. *'Fiat Libertas' Escape Line.*	The Netherlands. *1942 to June 1945*	Chap. 5	28 Jul 47*
FRAMPTON, *Miss* Violet Eva Alice. *S.R.N., S.C.M.* Nurse. *Bristol Maternity Hospital*	Bristol. *16/17 March 1941*	Chap. 2	30 May 41 *p. 3066*
FRASER, *Mrs.* Berthe Émilie. Perfumery owner and resistance worker.	Arras and area, France. *January 1941 to 1 September 1944*	Chap. 5	23 Jul 46 *p. 3795*
GARDNER, *Miss* Dorothy Kate. Probationer nurse. *Royal East Sussex Hospital.*	Hastings, Sussex. *7/8 April 1941*	Chap. 2	6 June 41 *p. 3199*
GAUTHIER, *Mlle.* Jeanette. 'Sussex' agent.	France. *February to August 1944*	Chap. 5	5 Sep 46*
GIBBS, *Miss* Mary Elizabeth. School teacher. *Faraday Primary School.*	Faraday, via Castlemaine, Victoria, Australia. *6/7 October 1972*	Chap. 7	23 Jan 73 *p. 1029*
GRANVILLE, *Miss* Mary Christine. (Maria Krystyna Gyzicki). *Women's Auxiliary Air Force Inter-Service Signals Unit, Middle East.*	Vercors, France. *6 July to August 1944*	Chap. 6	23 Jan 46*
GREAVES, *Lieut.* (Sister) Sheila Margaret. 206174. *Queen Alexandra's Imperial Military Nursing Service Reserve.*	Anzio, Italy. *14 March 1945*	Chap 4	23 Mar 45 *p. 1573*
de GREEF, *Mme.* Elvira. Organiser. *'Comet' Escape Line.*	France. *June 1941 to July 1944*	Chap. 5	8 Aug 45*
HEPBURN, *Mrs.* Bessie Jane. Attendant. *Ambulance Service.*	Aldeburgh, Suffolk. *8 July 1940*	Chap. 8	30 Sep 40 *p. 5768*
HOLLAND, *Miss* Freda. Night nurse. *Dellwood Nursing Home.*	Reading, Berkshire. *18 April 1954*	Chap. 8	22 Jun 54 *p. 3685*
HOLLYER, *Miss* Wendy Pauline. Telephonist. *A.R.P. Service.*	Croydon, Surrey *24 November 1940*	Chap. 1	7 Mar 41 *p. 1344*

HORNE, *Miss* Emma. *S.R.N., S.C.M.* Sister. *Coventry and Warwickshire Hospital.*	Coventry, Warwickshire. *8/9 April 1941*	Chap. 3	7 Jul 41 *p. 3894*
de JONGH, *Mlle.* Andrée. Leader. *'Comet' Escape Line.*	Belgium, France and Spain. *1941 to May 1945*	Chap. 5	8 Apr 45*
KATHIGASU, *Mrs.* Sybil. Nurse and housewife.	Ipoh, Malaya. *December 1941 to September 1945*	Chap. 6	14 Oct 47 *p. 4805*
KNEE, *Mrs.* Emily Alberta Mardon. Assistant night nurse. *City Hospital.*	Heavitree, Bristol. *4 May 1942*	Chap. 2	9 Oct 42 *p. 4391*
LEBLANC de CHOISAY, *Capte.* Laura. *Corps Auxiliaire Féminin.*	France. *June 1941 to September 1944*	Chap. 5	30 Jul 47*
McGOVERN, *Miss* Catherine. *A.R.R.C., S.R.N.* Assistant Matron. *Royal Chest Hospital.*	Islington, London. *11 September 1940*	Chap. 1	17 Jan 41 *p. 330*
McNAIRN, *Dr.* Alison Jean. *M.B., B.S.* Assistant Medical Officer. *City General Hospital.*	Plymouth, Devon. *20 March 1941*	Chap. 2	27 Jun 41 *p. 3647*
MALONI, *Mrs.* Belini. Children's nurse. *Ballybush Farm.*	Chingola, Northern Rhodesia. *10 December 1940*	Chap. 8	10 Apr 62 *p. 2918*
MARMION, *Miss* Patricia. Staff nurse. *Royal Chest Hospital.*	Islington, London. *11 September 1940*	Chap. 1	17 Jan 41 *p. 330*
NEWMAN, *Miss* Mary Sible Joyce. Assistant nurse. *Borough Medical Services.*	Bitterne, Southampton. *23 November 1940*	Chap. 2	21 Feb 41 *p. 1060*
OWEN, *Miss* Elizabeth May. Stewardess. *Fishguard and Rosslare Railway. S.S. St. Patrick.*	Off Strumble Head, Fishguard, Pembrokeshire. *13 June 1941*	Chap. 2	23 Sep 41 *p. 5497*
PARROTT, *Mrs.* Kathleen Flora. Woman Police Constable. *Metropolitan Police.*	Croydon, Surrey. *23 April 1955*	Chap. 7	14 Jun 55 *p. 3450*

PATTERSON, *Mrs.* Marion. Senior fire guard. *A.R.P. Service.*	Aberdeen, Aberdeenshire. *7 August 1942*	Chap. 3	4 Dec 42 *p. 5293*
PERKINS, *Miss* Marjorie Eileen. Works nurse. *Pattison and Hobourne Ltd.*	Coventry, Warwickshire. *14/15 November 1940*	Chap. 3	7 Feb 41 *p. 739*
QUINN, *Miss* Betty. Cadet Corporal. *St. John Ambulance Brigade.*	Coventry, Warwickshire. *19 October 1940*	Chap. 3	13 Dec 40 *p. 7019*
RATTENBURY, *Miss* Grace. *W.V.S.* and Organiser *Invalid Children's Aid Association.*	Rotherhithe, London. *7 September 1940*	Chap. 1	7 Feb 41 *p. 739*
REID, *Miss* Violet Eleanor. Junior nurse. *Montrose Royal Asylum.*	Montrose, Angus. *2 October 1940*	Chap. 3	15 Nov 40 *p. 6611*
RICHARDS, *L.Cpl.* Margaret Emma. W/119306. *Auxiliary Territorial Service.*	Saxelbye, Leicestershire. *14 January 1948*	Chap. 8	2 Jul 48 *p. 3825*
RODRIGUEZ, *Miss* Helen. Matron. *Civil Hospital.*	Taunggyi, Burma. *10 to 20 April 1942*	Chap. 4	8 May 42 *p. 2015*
ROSSER, *Miss* Ruby Eirlys Megan. *S.R.N.* Staff nurse. *Grove Park Hospital.*	Grove Park, London. *19 November 1940*	Chap. 1	24 Apr 41 *p. 2338*
SAVAGE, *Lieut.* (Sister) Ellen. NFX 76584. *Australian Army Nursing Service.* A.H.S. *Centaur.*	Off Brisbane, Queensland, Australia. *13 May 1943*	Chap. 8	25 Aug 44 *p. 3941*
SJØBERG, *2/Lieut.* Liv. (Liv Grannes) *Norwegian Armed Forces.*	Mosjøen, Norway. *July 1940 to 1942*	Chap. 5	22 Jul 46*
STEELE, *Miss* Maude. Supervising Telephonist. *General Post Office.*	Sherborne, Dorset. *30 September 1940*	Chap. 2	3 Jan 41 *p. 47*
STEVENS, *Miss* Elsie Lillian. Assistant matron. *Bristol Maternity Hospital.*	Bristol. *16/17 March 1941*	Chap. 2	30 Nov 41 *p. 3066*
STRAW, *Miss* Sonia Vera Carlyle. Air raid warden. *A.R.P. Service.*	Caterham, Surrey. *1 September 1940*	Chap. 1	30 Sep 40 *p. 5769*

TANNER, *Miss* Gillian Kluane. Auxiliary. *Women's Auxiliary Fire Service.*	Bermondsey, London. *30 September 1940*	Chap. 2	31 Jan 41 *p. 610*
THOMAS, *Miss* Evalyn Gertrude. Matron. *West Bromwich and District General Hospital.*	West Bromwich, Warwickshire. *19 November 1940*	Chap. 3	14 Feb 41 *p. 873*
THOMAS, *Miss* Mary Felicia. Nurse. *A.R.P. Casualty Service.*	Plumstead, London. *7 and 20 September 1940*	Chap. 1	24 Jan 41 *p. 483*
TURNER, *Miss* Aileen Ruth. Senior assistant nurse. *Grove Park Hospital.*	Grove Park, London. *19 November 1940*	Chap. 1	9 May 41 *p. 2639*
VEARNECOMBE, *Miss* Marjorie.	West Worlington, Crediton, Devon. *22 June 1951*	Chap. 7	25 Sept 51 *p. 4990*
WAKE, *Miss* Nancy Grace Augusta. Ensign. *First Aid Nursing Yeomanry.*	Auvergne, France. *29 April to September 1944*	Chap. 6	17 Jul 45 *p. 3676*
WALSH, *Mrs.* Francis. School teacher. *Big Springs School.*	Calgary, Alberta, Canada. *10 November 1941*	Chap. 8	11 Jun 42 *p. 2533*
WHITE, *Miss* Dorothy May. V.A.D. *British Red Cross Society.*	Colegate, Sussex. *9 September 1940*	Chap. 2	31 Jan 41 *p. 610*
YOUNG, *Miss* Marion. Nurse. *Dundee Royal Infirmary.*	Dundee, Angus. *1 November 1967*	Chap. 7	14 May 68 *p. 5453*

Names are as published in London Gazette Supplement or citation.

* Date of approval – not published in *London Gazette Supplement.*

† First published in *New Zealand Gazette* dated 19 December 1991.

Sources

Bibliography

BENSEMANN, Paul, *Tragedy at Aramoana*. Cape Catley Ltd. New Zealand 1991

BERWICK SAYERS, W.C. (Ed), *Croydon And The Second World War*. The Croydon Corporation 1949

BRADDON, Russell, *Nancy Wake*. Cassell & Co. Ltd. London 1956

CASKIE, Dr Donald C., *The Tartan Pimpernel*. Oldbourne Book Co. Ltd. London 1957

COOPER, Alan W., *Free to Fight Again*. William Kimber. London 1988

CRUICKSHANK, Charles, *S.O.E. in Scandinavia*. OUP Oxford 1986

CURNOCK, George C. (Ed), *Hospitals Under Fire*. George Allen & Unwin Ltd. London 1941

DEMARNE, Cyril, OBE, *The London Blitz*. Battle of Britain Prints International Ltd. London 1991

FIELDING, Xan, *Hide and Seek*. Secker & Warburg. London 1951

FITZGIBBON, Constantine, *The Blitz*. Wingate. London 1966

FOOT, M.R.D., *S.O.E. In France*. HMSO London 1966

FOOT, M.R.D., *Six Faces of Courage*. Eyre Methuen. London 1978

FOOT, M.R.D. & LANGLEY, J.M., *M.I.9. Escape and Evasion 1939–1945*. The Bodley Head. London.

GAWLER, Jim, *Lloyd's Medals 1836–1945*. Hart Publishing. Toronto 1989

GOLDSMITH, John, *Accidental Agent*. Leo Cooper. London 1971

HARRISON, Tom, *Living Through The Blitz*. Collins. London. 1976

HMSO, *Front Line*. HMSO London 1942

HOCKING, Charles F.L.A., *Dictionary of Disasters at Sea during the Age of Steam 1829–1962*. Lloyd's Register of Shipping. London 1964

HOWARTH, Patrick, *Undercover*. Routledge & Kegan Paul. London 1980

JACKETT, Sam, *Heroes of Scotland Yard*. Robert Hale. London 1965

JACKSON, Robert, *Heroines of World War II*. Arthur Barker Ltd, London

KATHIGASU, Sybil, *No Dram of Mercy*. OUP (Singapore). Singapore 1983

LANGLEY, Lt.Col. J.M., *Fight Another Day*. Collins. London 1974

LONG, Helen, *Safe Houses Are Dangerous*. William Kimber. London 1985

LONGMATE, Norman, *Air Raid – The Bombing of Coventry 1940*. Hutchinson. London 1957

MASSON, Madelaine, *Christine*. Hamish Hamilton. London 1975

MASTERS, David, *In Peril on the Sea*. The Cresset Press. London 1975

NEAVE, Airey, *Little Cyclone*. Hodder & Stoughton Ltd. London 1954

NEAVE, Airey, *Saturday at M.I.9*. Hodder & Stoughton Ltd, London 1967

O'BRIEN, Bill, *Aromoana. Twenty-two Hours of Terror*. Penguin Books (NZ) Ltd. 1991

PIGGOTT, Julia, *Queen Alexandra's Royal Army Nursing Corps*. Leo Cooper. London

RODRIGUEZ, Helen, *Helen of Burma*. Collins. London 1983

ROOSENBURG, Henrietta, *The Walls Came Tumbling Down*. Secker & Warburg Ltd. London 1957

SCARLETT, R.J., *Under Hazardous Circumstances*. Naval & Military Press. Dallington 1992

SPILLER, H.J., DFM, *Ticket To Freedom*. William Kimber. London 1988

TWYFORD, H.P., *It Came to Our Door*. Underhill (Plymouth). Plymouth 1945

WAKE, Nancy, *The White Mouse*. Macmillan Co. (Australia). Melbourne 1985

WALLINGTON, Neil, *Firemen at War*. David & Charles. Newton Abbot 1981

Official Histories

WALKER, A., Official history – Medical Services R.A.N. and R.A.A.F. Australia in the War 1939–45. Australian War Memorial 1961

WALKER, A., Official History – Middle East and Far East. Australian War Memorial 1961

HERMON, Gill, The Royal Australian Navy, 1939–1942.

Official Publications

The *London Gazette*, various dates

The *New Zealand Gazette*, various dates

The Medical Directory, various dates

The Medical Register, various dates

Australian Army Gradation List, various dates

Public Record Office files:

- AIR 2 series
- ADM 199 series
- FO 372 series
- HO 250 series